A PHILOSOPHER LOOKS AT WORK

Is work as we know it disappearing? And if so why should we care? These questions are explored by Raymond Geuss in this compact but sweeping survey which integrates conceptual analysis, historical reflection, autobiography, and social commentary. Geuss explores our concept of work and its origins in industrial production, the incentives and compulsions which societies use to get us to work, and the powerful hold which the work-ethic has over so many of us. He also looks at dissatisfaction with work – which is as old as work itself – and at various radical proposals for doing away with it, and at the seemingly irreversible growth of unemployment as a result of mechanisation. His book will interest anyone who wishes to understand the place of work in our world. This new series offers short and personal perspectives by expert thinkers on topics that we all encounter in our everyday lives.

RAYMOND GEUSS is Professor Emeritus of Philosophy at the University of Cambridge. He is the author of over a dozen books on political and critical theory, ethics, and the history of philosophy, including *The Idea of a Critical Theory* (Cambridge, 1981), *History and Illusion in Politics* (Cambridge, 2001), *Changing the Subject* (2017), and *Who Needs a World View?* (2020).

T0139701

A Philosopher Looks at

In this series, philosophers offer a personal and philosophical exploration of a topic of general interest.

Books in the series

A PHILOSOPHER LOOKS AT

WORK

RAYMOND GEUSS

CAMBRIDGE
UNIVERSITY PRESS

CAMBRIDGE
UNIVERSITY PRESS

University Printing House, Cambridge CB2 8BS, United Kingdom

One Liberty Plaza, 20th Floor, New York, NY 10006, USA

477 Williamstown Road, Port Melbourne, VIC 3207, Australia

314–321, 3rd Floor, Plot 3, Splendor Forum, Jasola District Centre, New Delhi – 110025, India

79 Anson Road, #06–04/06, Singapore 079906

Cambridge University Press is part of the University of Cambridge.

It furthers the University's mission by disseminating knowledge in the pursuit of education, learning, and research at the highest international levels of excellence.

www.cambridge.org
Information on this title: www.cambridge.org/9781108930611
DOI: 10.1017/9781108946216

© Raymond Geuss 2021

First published 2021

Printed in the United Kingdom by TJ Books Limited, Padstow Cornwall

A catalogue record for this publication is available from the British Library.

ISBN 978-1-108-93061-1 Paperback

CONTENTS

CONTENTS

In the summer of 1953, when I was six years old, my family moved to a settlement about 20 miles north of Philadelphia built for workers in the Fairless Works of US Steel. The newly constructed Works stood on a muddy peninsula in the Delaware River which, at that point, separates Pennsylvania from New Jersey. My father was one of the first workers recruited. In the 1960s and early 1970s the plant directly employed 8,000 workers, and then there were perhaps a further 5,000 employed in the subsidiary industrial plants that clustered around the main works. To serve the large number of new workers who moved into the area around the steel mill, often from great distances, the Catholic Church created several new parishes, with attached schools. We went to mass at the Church of St Joseph the Worker, and I went to the parochial school there. The dedication of the parish to St Joseph, specifically in his aspect as a man who worked with his hands, gave a religious sanction to the role that all of us were, it was assumed, going to be called upon to play in life – all of the boys, at any rate. Activity in the plant began to decline in 1975 when the government of Venezuela nationalised the mining of iron ore – the plant had been built to process iron ore mined for practically nothing in Venezuela, imported through the port of Philadelphia, and then sent by barge upriver to the Fairless Works. US Steel got an enormous government grant to 'modernise' in 1981, but it used the money to speculate, which it did badly, and it seemed to lose interest in the production of steel. The last forty workers, who were still operating some remaining machines in one dark corner of the plant, were made redundant in 1988. St Joseph the Worker parish was disbanded. In 2017 the church building, the school, the rectory, and the convent for the nuns who taught in the school were torn down, and on the site a local developer built a retirement community.

The story I have just recounted is a banal one, and variants of it could be told by millions of people in the older industrialised countries. My desire to write this book arises in part out of a desire to understand this part of my own history, which is parallel to that of a large number of people in Western societies. What was that 'work' around which our lives were supposed to be centred? What role did it actually play in our lives? How have things changed? Is it possible to have any well supported expectations about what role work will play in the future? This is a philosophical project because at least one of the traditional aspirations of philosophy since Socrates has been to come to self-knowledge, which includes knowledge of one's location in the world, in history, in the present, and in the various possible futures. To locate oneself and one's experience in society is to determine their place in a nexus of facts, but also of hopes, aspirations, expectations, values, and fears which form the framework within which individuals and groups conduct their lives. It is important not to confuse an aspiration or a fear with a reality, but equally no one can understand a society without taking account of its conceptions of heaven and of which hell holds the greatest terror for it.

Unfortunately, the existing state of recent philosophy makes it necessary to range more broadly if one wishes to treat the topic of work at all adequately. There is certainly no guarantee that philosophy – in the narrow academic way the discipline is now practised – gives any kind of special access to or provides a particularly good understanding of the phenomenon of work. Frankly, work has not received much treatment from philosophers, recently, at any rate. Partly, I suspect, this is for political reasons. The most sustained body of theoretical reflection on work and associated phenomena was that produced during the nineteenth and twentieth centuries by people who can all be reasonably called 'socialists' (in the broadest possible sense of that term), with a sprinkling of anarchists in the mix. The collapse of the Soviet Union in 1989 was taken by many, whether correctly or incorrectly, to represent a general refutation of the whole way of proceeding that was characteristic of this group of thinkers, and established Western political, business, and commercial interests, for obvious reasons, welcomed this development. In that kind of atmosphere it would have required very significant amounts of initiative, independent-mindedness, and concentration to write on this topic.

In the 1970s something changed, or at least began to change, in the structure of work in Western countries, and also, much more gradually (because superstructural inertia is great), in our conception of work. The centrality of a certain paradigm of our society began to be undermined. It began to seem no longer an obvious fact of nature that very large portions of the population would always have to be engaged in some kind of strenuous industrial labour, basically something like factory work, for most of their adult lives.

Two factors were involved in this. The first was the mechanisation and automation of work processes, which led to an enormous reduction in the portion of the population engaged in industrial manufacturing. To some extent this was accompanied by a rise in what are called the 'service industries'. Service industries are not really like old-style factory work in several relevant respects. Manufacturing was characteristically bashing metal, or otherwise intervening in natural processes, whereas many of the service industries were directed at the management, organisation, or cultivation of people. The changes in the work process – more administration, catering, facilitation, promotion, marketing, book-keeping relative to the amount of direct production of objects – had far-reaching effects on people's conceptions of their own lives and how they needed to live them.

Fabrics, steel, and manufactured objects were still needed, however, and so a second factor was the massive outsourcing of industrial production away from national centres to the peripheries and then out, principally to Asia. This movement was, of course, stronger in some countries than in others – much stronger, for instance, in the UK than in Germany. This meant that by the 1990s industrial work in the West had become much less central and much less visible than it had been, so that the cliché about a post-industrial age had some validity. This had a significant effect on our politics, for instance in weakening the power of labour unions.

In fact, somewhat to my surprise, as I was writing this book I began to become increasingly convinced that it really belongs not so much to the genre of 'treatment of current events' as to that of historical anthropology. It gives a snapshot of what is now, for us, a world of work that is quickly passing away, if not already completely gone. The whole discussion of work in terms of exertion, needs, the work-ethic, objectivity, and the rest no longer reflects the realities of a world in which the gig economy is part of the way of life. Equally archaic is the idea that in society more or less everyone except a handful of tremendously privileged people will have to work most of the time, and that this fact will be crucial in structuring their lives. I merely mention the fact that pensioners like me, in contrast to previous ages, now constitute a not insignificant proportion of the population. Maybe pensioners once did work, but they are not now part of the active work-force, even if they dabble in minor forms of remunerated activity. The prospect that many more people than before can expect ten or more years of life during which the necessity to work is suspended, because of pensions, savings, perhaps even investments, and various public forms of support, makes a big social difference. That these pensions may be less than fully adequate for many and that public support is constantly threatened by governmental action is perfectly true and by no means unimportant, but it is not relevant to the point I am trying to make here.

For a brief moment in the 1960s, those of us who lived through that period could get a glimpse of a world without the compulsion to work and constant anxiety about finding employment. When I went to university in 1963, I had a scholarship to pay my fees and so needed money only for living expenses, which in my case meant primarily expensive, foreign books. This was the (last) real boom period of the American economy, and I could earn enough working in a steel mill for six weeks in the summer to fund myself for a year or more. Such unskilled, well-paid jobs were readily available; it was always possible to get one of them if you absolutely needed money. One did, then, still need occasionally to go to work, but only when the need was real and pressing, and this did not preoccupy anyone or serve as a context of definition for a life. Under such conditions, spending six weeks at relatively strenuous work once a year did not seem much, not even during the one summer when I scrubbed the walls of the plant's canteen every day in temperatures of well over 40 °C, only to arrive back the next morning to find them freshly covered with a new thick layer of condensed and congealed cooking oil, industrial grease, coal and iron dust, dead flies, and who knows what. However, working an eight-hour day for six weeks doing something different was such a short stint that it was almost like a break. The momentary image in the mid 1960s of the demotion of work in a post-scarcity world did not survive the end of that particular economic boom – by the end of the 1980s the steel mill where my father (and I) had worked was closed for good. In addition, the publication of *The Limits to Growth*, the Report of the Club of Rome, in 1972 meant that at any rate some of the more naive ideas about the possibility of unlimited increase in industrial activity leading to a state of post-scarcity became untenable. If it looked for a very brief moment as if we were going to break through to a society that would, by virtue of being in some sense beyond scarcity, relegate necessary work to a very subordinate position in human life, the prospectus now was for a society that was certainly not beyond scarcity, but in which nevertheless work in the traditional sense was increasingly disappearing. The traditional job would be a thing of the past and, in addition, most of the population would have been rendered permanently unemployable as a result of automation.

Although the world of traditional work is largely gone, it continues to have an exceedingly strong hold on the way in which people think about work and life. Conceptual inertia means that if we want to understand our present, this is (part of) what we must try to deal with. In the final chapter of this book I engage in some speculation about possible futures, but this is not intended to do anything other than to suggest some possibilities for further reflection.

I would like to thank Brian O'Connor, Lorna Finlayson, and Richard Raatzsch for reading and providing me with very helpful comments on early versions of the text, and Martin Bauer, Zeev Emmerich, and Peter Garnsey for discussions of the topics treated here. Hilary Gaskin originally commissioned me to write this book, and she has read and commented on successive drafts with her usual acuity. I owe her a great debt of gratitude for the improvements of individual passages which she introduced throughout and for her many good suggestions about the general direction of the argument.

1   What Is Work?

'We all need to work,' my mother would say in that tone which, while purporting to enunciate an obvious truth that needed no support and would brook no argument, actually contained a threat.

However, she seemed to be right. My maternal grandfather operated a loom in a textile mill in West Philadelphia; my paternal grandfather had been a baker, and then he worked on the railway. In the 1940s one of my paternal uncles married a woman who inherited a farm in southern Indiana, which they worked (eventually together with their five children). In the 1940s the farm was not completely self-sufficient, because the family could not live solely on what they produced themselves; they produced mostly for sale in the market, however, yields and prices were such as to allow my uncle and his family to live from selling what they produced without taking other employment. Increasingly, however, during the 1960s, the economic situation changed, so that in addition to his work on the farm my uncle needed to find a job as an industrial cleaner in a pharmaceutical plant in town. As time went on, the work in town became more and more important. My father was a mechanic at the Fairless Works of US Steel in Eastern Pennsylvania; his job was to repair the diesel locomotives and overhead magnetic cranes that were used to transport ore, iron, and steel from one part of the steel mill to another.

My grandmother spent all day cleaning the house, washing clothing, and cooking, and my mother worked as a typist, filing clerk, stenographer, and secretary in various companies that bought and sold things. I myself had a series of summer jobs in the steel mill during the 1960s, and also worked for one summer as a 'freight-agent' ('*Frachtagent*') in the Rhein/Main Airport in Frankfurt am Main, Germany. Between starting permanent full-time employment in 1971 and my retirement in 2014, I spent my entire working life teaching, examining, producing reports and evaluations, and writing books and articles. We use the same general word, 'work', for all these activities, despite their manifest differences. Is it reasonable for us to do this? What is this activity we call 'work'? I would like to begin by discussing some of the sorts of things we spontaneously say (and think) about work and some of the things we contrast it with, such as relaxation, leisure, play, idleness, unemployment, vacation/holiday, and retirement.

Our conception of work is modelled, in the first instance, on industrial labour of the kind my father and grandfather did. We tend to think of work as a clear, simple, self-evident concept with which anyone will be familiar, but if one thinks about the things people tend to say about work, they suggest that it is more complicated, and that people at least partly see that. For instance, I can clearly recall three rather different kinds of things my father used repeatedly to say about work, which suggested at the very least that the concept as he used it had an interesting internal articulation or referred to different dimensions of human action, although he himself may not have been absolutely clear about this. Once a day he would eat a very heavy meal, and he would often remark that he needed to eat a lot of nourishing food to 'keep my strength up for work'. So work was an activity that required exertion; it was different from idleness (for which one did not have to keep one's strength up), and what it required was not easy. Often, after eating, just before his shift started, he would announce while leaving the house that he 'had to go to work now', sometimes adding to this that he needed 'to go and earn a living'. This suggested, first, that 'work' was something distinct from the rest of life, involving, in his case, going off to a separate area, the steel mill, which was a large space surrounded by metal-mesh fences, patrolled by a private security force, and comprising several large buildings connected by roads and lengths of railway track. Going there was not a choice or something he necessarily wanted to do; it was a matter of necessity: he 'had' to go. The third thing he would say was in a way the most striking: in the case of any behaviour he considered to be overly fussy and fastidious, the presentation of excuses, appeal to personal preferences or attitudes, or instances of excessively complex ratiocination, he would remark that 'we work on a production basis here'. This last remark was derived, I discovered, from what his foreman at the steel mill used to say to all the men in his section. What it meant was that no amount of reasoning, talk, or moral scruples really had any standing when it came to work; only the quality (and especially quantity) of the finished product counted. Work was something concerned with what was 'out there' in the real world, visible to all, countable and assessable, not a matter of mere opinion or a part of the drama of anyone's inner sphere. The steel mill even produced pencils bearing the inscription *US Steel: Knowing's not enough!* If even knowing was not enough (compared with demonstrable output), a fortiori, any kind of *attitude* a worker might have to what he or she did was irrelevant. Some of these pencils always found their way into our house. When I myself started work at the steel mill I realised that the motto in that pithy inscription was part of the company's *safety* policy, the idea being that accidents were not the company's responsibility, but were all the result of carelessness on the part of the workers: they 'knew' they should wear their helmets and steel-tipped shoes at all times, but it was hot in a steel mill in Pennsylvania in August and the steel-tipped shoes and helmets were uncomfortable. My father, however, did not interpret the motto on the pencil in this narrow and specific way. He took it to indicate that 'work' was a separate domain governed by its own objective internal standards, and that not even '*knowing*', the paradigm of a serious, well-grounded, but merely mental attitude toward the world, had any special standing in comparison with these imperative standards. Work was the final framework and the model for all of human life. The 'work' referred to in the phrase 'we work on a production basis' was in fact the work of human living in all its forms and varieties. Human life as a whole should be just as free of posturing, fancy reasoning, excessive expression of feelings etc. as work in the steel mill was. One of the reasons my father liked the production ethos of his job was that, as long as he kept the relevant locomotives and cranes running, it was nobody's business what he ate, what he thought, what he liked or did not like, what his personal habits were, or what attitude he had toward his work or management. Work was serious, life was serious, and the ethos of steel production was the ideal to which one should aspire in all respects and all domains, if one wished to be a serious person.

I take these three sayings of my father to illustrate three important aspects of our most usual conception of work:

(a) it is a process that requires expenditure of energy and is strenuous: the product is not produced effortlessly or by magic, but by *human* exertion (in particular the exertion of the individual or a group of individuals who are said to be working)
(b) it is a necessity of life
(c) it has an external produced product that can be measured and evaluated independently of anything one might know about the process through which that product came to be or the people who made it (I'll call this for short 'objectivity' in one sense of that highly ambiguous term).

In paradigmatic cases of what we, people in the West at the beginning of the twenty-first century, call 'work' these three elements are all present. Work in the full-blown generally accepted sense will contain all three elements as part of an integrated whole. However, these three strands do not seem always *necessarily* to go together; one can imagine them as being separate and separately instantiated. Even in some cases that are familiar to us from our everyday experience this is true, and it certainly is true if one looks at how human activity has been structured historically. If only one or two, but not all three, strands are not co-present in a certain class of cases, it will be a matter of judgement, convention, tradition, historical accident, and individual initiative whether or not we call the activity 'work'. Guide dogs leading the blind in Britain often carry a sign reading 'Guide dog working', or sometimes 'Don't distract me, I'm working'; should the dog be paid for this work? Can a robot exert himself (or herself)? If a visit to a park calms office workers down so that they can return to work reinvigorated, is the park a work place? Could a dog, a robot, or a park join a labour union? We are not forced by the logic of our concepts to answer these questions one way or the other. Concepts are always open-ended. This does not mean that what counts as work is a mere matter of arbitrary decision. It does mean that how far metaphorical extensions will reach and to what extent they will embed themselves in our daily lives and become literally true is unpredictable. That 'the robot works' is literally true might be easily granted given that 'robot' comes from a common Slavic root that means 'work', but is 'guide dog working' a metaphor or not? If not, when did it become literally, rather than metaphorically, true? A wide variety of historical, linguistic, political, social, literary, and other contextual factors and forces is involved in establishing something as a form of work. How these factors will in fact play themselves out in any concrete situation in the future is not random, but it is also not strictly predictable.

The three components just mentioned constitute, I submit, the central core of our usual conception of work, but there are some other further aspects that are not quite as essential, but which also play an important if more subordinate role in the way we think about work. My father used the expression 'go (out) to work' completely unselfconsciously. That is, work was

(d) a distinct and almost self-contained activity, and thus was most appropriately conducted in its own separate space, a factory or garage, or mill (or eventually office) in order that it not be confused with anything else.

He, of course, realised that some people worked from home – the odd craftsman, perhaps, like the various men who had a small business repairing cars in their own garages. Even such people, however, would be generally assumed to have their own work-space. Furthermore, he also realised that some people liked their work, or even could combine certain kinds of work with lightheartedness, but that was an accident, a lucky break for the person who liked doing what had in any case to be done. Levity, jokiness, good humour were almost always in tension with the underlying idea of working. Practical jokes, in particular, in the steel mill were extremely dangerous, a cause of innumerable accidents. Thus

(e) work was almost invariably distinct from what one might do for fun, for pleasure, or as a joke. It was paradigmatically serious.

Finally, there was a tacit assumption that ran through everything my father said and thought, which was absolutely fundamental and was really so self-evident that it did not need to be separately expressed:

(f) work is archetypically activity for which you receive pay in the form of money; it is monetarised.

Again, it was not as if my father forgot that one of his brothers did a lot of work, and hard work, on his farm, for which he certainly did not receive cash from anyone – he was growing things for his own and his family's consumption. It was just that that was construed as a kind of subsidiary or subordinate phenomenon. Raising crops for one's own consumption was something to be understood in the final context of paid work, because if you ate what you grew yourself, you didn't have to buy it. Working for cash, raising crops to sell (and then working as a cleaner), was the main event around which everything else had to be finally grouped and relative to which it had to be construed.

The more seriously one takes (d) and (f), the more housework, characteristically done by women, will be taken to be a marginal phenomenon, because, although it eminently satisfies criteria (a), (b) and (c), it is usually unpaid and usually does not take place as a separate and distinct activity (in the sense intended in (d)).

The three elements of work which I have listed above do not constitute anything like a formal definition of work, nor does one get such a definition if one adds the further three features. Rather they point to, and mark out in a vague and approximate way, a kind of discursive territory within which discussion of work is conducted. Before continuing this discussion, though, it would make sense to try to clarify to a slightly greater extent the three main elements in our conception.

Exertion

Physical and Moral Exertion

To work is to do something strenuous. To call something 'strenuous' means in the first instance that it requires someone to exercise their muscles continuously and intensely, as normal people would do in moving rocks from one place to another all day long, rowing a boat, or threshing grain.

Actually, there seem to be two components to this: first, a strictly physical or technical aspect, but also a second 'moral' aspect. To start with the technical sense, 'work' was used in physics and engineering originally to refer to the amount of weight a given animal can raise to a certain height. One can then extend the concept by applying it not just to how much a whole given animal, such as a horse, can lift how far, but also to how much a particular human muscle group can lift. Eventually the concept of 'work' can be formalised in physics and detached from the idea of an animal moving or lifting something, so that the work which a boiler or engine does can be defined abstractly as the product of force exerted and distance. In any case, what is important is that work can be measured strictly by its external result: the weight moved can be externally measured and the height to which it is raised can also be measured, and between them they determine what the 'work' is. How much work one human being can do is then partly a matter of natural endowment: a horse can in general raise a heavier weight than an unaided human can. Partly, however, it is also a matter of nutrition and training. An able-bodied adult who is well nourished and lifts weights regularly will, in general, eventually, be able to life heavier weights further than a comparable adult who has no training. A human job is strenuous if it requires a certain amount of physical work in this sense of 'work', the strict one employed in engineering.

There is, however, also a second way in which we use the word 'strenuous'. One can call this the 'moral' sense (in the slightly old-fashioned sense of 'moral' which is often used by philosophers). 'Strenuous' here is an adjective designating how much effort I can and do 'force myself to make'. Animals, and particularly humans, can 'try harder' (or, alternatively, 'slack off'). We can try to make them try harder, for instance by whipping them, something that used regularly to be done to animals like horses and to human slaves. How hard I have to try to attain a certain result will be relative to my natural physical and psychological endowments and my state of training. There may be a weight I can lift only with great exertion – by trying very hard – but which a person naturally stronger or in better training than me would lift without any special difficulty. Occasionally we have the experience of a human, A, who is inherently capable of less work than some other human, B, but who nevertheless regularly surpasses B in measurable work. B, for instance, is physically much stronger than A, and he *could, if he really exerted himself,* move a much greater weight of stone a greater distance during his work-shift, but A forces himself to make greater efforts during the shift and actually moves more stone further than B does. One might think of the distinction as illustrated in the slight differences in the meaning of 'work'. Say that both A and B have a quota of 500 stones weighing 10 kilos each to move a distance of three metres each during a given time. During that time B moves 1,000 stones over the distance, and A only 500. We might say

(a) B did more work (in the engineering sense) than A did

but

(b) A had to work harder (in the moral sense) to fulfil the quota than B did.

These two statements are perfectly compatible with each other.

Of course, there can be a number of different reasons for discrepancies, even a systematic recurring discrepancy, between the amount of actual work (in the engineering sense) which a given individual (or group) performs and what he, she, or they are in principle capable of. One such reason is that the person whose work we are considering is suffering from the condition we call laziness, lack of application, failure to exert oneself.

Contrary to the ethos of steel production which so impressed my father, some people have an inclination to valorise effort highly, even in the absence of any corresponding objective result. This moralising attitude sometimes infects discussion of merit or desert. It can cut both ways. My father's foreman thought that only production was important, in that no amount of effort or good will could compensate for deficiencies in the measurable amount of work (in the engineering sense). In addition, lots of religious leaders, teachers, moralists, and, for that matter, ordinary humans tend to have suspicions about any form of apparently lazy behaviour. They might even be inclined to think that a supremely gifted person who is performing huge amounts of work effortlessly is not 'really' working. It turns out that it is entirely possible in some contexts to avoid such moralising attitudes, but it is extremely hard to do this consistently in all cases and contexts. One great problem is that effort (as opposed to actual performance) is very difficult to measure, and there is no consensus on how to evaluate its weight relative to other factors in a final assessment of some work.

So full-blown work is, in a typical case, strenuous, both in the engineering and in the moral sense. Up to this point, it has been assumed that the activity that is called strenuous is a physical activity of some sort – raising of weights, moving of objects, pulling things along, or something like that – but eventually, words like 'exertion', 'effort', and 'strenuous' can have their meanings extended to encompass what are taken to be comparable mental phenomena, such as solving a complicated equation which requires a high degree of concentration and persistence in the use of mental powers that are construed as being like the power of our physical muscles. So there is 'manual' and 'mental' work (sometimes called 'work of the hands' and 'work of the head' in the Marxist tradition). Eventually, one might extend the concept of 'work' to include not simply more or less straightforwardly mental activities – book-keeping, stenography, simultaneous translation, processing large amounts of data, or solving complex formal problems – that are clearly strenuous and require high degrees of concentration, but even to more ethereal spheres such as marriage-counselling, acting, facilitating. Given that it is difficult enough to see where natural ability and training end and where effort begins in the case of physical or manual work, the difficulty of applying these distinctions to cases of work of the head, the mind, or the spirit increases exponentially, so assessing the work done gets even more difficult.

Idleness, Play, Holiday, Retirement

To say that work is a strenuous activity could mean to say it is inherently disagreeable, or unpleasant to the person who performs it, because we might think that people don't naturally like to have to strain their muscles. There are at least four other human states that are regularly contrasted with 'work', and seeing how these contrasts are constructed will give the concept of 'work' more contour. First, if I am not engaged in any particular activity at all, then I am clearly not working, unless I am a life-model for an artist. If the lack of activity is voluntary, I am idling; if the lack of activity is a relatively brief period between two periods of work and is construed as a necessary part of a process by which I regain my strength after exertion in order to work again, I am resting; if my lack of work is involuntary I am unemployed (or perhaps disabled, or both). Another possibility is that I am not inactive, but am doing something, perhaps vigorously, which does not count as work – for instance, I am playing a game. Much human play (which in many contexts is strictly distinguished from work) can be highly strenuous. Many organised sports, which large numbers of people play 'for the fun of it', require very high levels of exertion. Playing rugby is much more strenuous than discharging several of the jobs which I successively had at the steel mill and all of which counted as 'work'. Whether an activity is work or play is something that depends partly on the wider context and cannot always be determined by direct inspection of the action in question alone. There are professional rugby players for whom this is a job, but for most of those who play it is not work. This example also shows that 'work' in some contexts is not a physical or biological, but a specifically *social*, category.

The professional and the amateur rugby players may engage on the field in activities that are observationally virtually indistinguishable. What makes this activity 'work' for the professional is the specific complex matrix of social relations within which the activity is embedded, especially, of course, the fact that rugby is for the professional a (virtually) full-time activity for which he is remunerated and by which he earns his living, (f) in the list above.

A third possibility is that, as I might say, I am 'on holiday' (having a break, taking a vacation) during a brief period which I construe as a short interruption of a much longer period of sustained work. During such a period I may be free to rest and do nothing, to play, or to engage in various other non-work activities. It is up to me, within limits, how I will spend my holiday, whereas work is typically subject to necessity, a necessity imposed by nature, which means in most cases by an employer, or in some cases by myself in response to a perceived natural necessity.

Finally, I may once have worked consistently for a relatively long time, but now I decide permanently to stop. This may be because of age, or disability, or because I think I have accumulated enough entitlements to support myself for the rest of my life without working any more, or in principle for no particular reason (although this last is rather uncommon). Then I say I have 'retired'. This is different from being compelled permanently to stop working for some reason; then I have not retired, I have been forcibly retired. Thus at the end of the First and Second World Wars women who had certain kinds of jobs that were otherwise considered to be men's jobs were dismissed en masse, and until very recently people who were keen to continue to work and still perfectly capable of doing what was necessary were forcibly retired at some arbitrary age.

Necessity

The 'necessity' of work that is in question here is not logical necessity. Rather, work is a necessity relative to a certain set of goals which we think we can assume that all humans have. These goals include mere biological survival, but go significantly beyond that. Even a family in complete destitution may biologically survive. What we attribute to people is the need to lead a life which satisfies at least the minimal conditions of what they take to be a *human* life, where that is culturally defined; sometimes this is called a 'decent' life. My father, mother, sister, and I could probably have survived on

the streets of Philadelphia for a while through some combination of scavenging, theft, odd-jobbery, begging, and
various other forms of charity, so the necessity to work
was a need to avoid a culturally unacceptable outcome like
this rather than immediate physical demise. Standards of
what counts as an acceptable decent life are not just socially
constituted but have varied enormously through time and in
different places. In many societies people will simply not eat
certain perfectly nutritious and widely available food for a
variety of social, cultural, and religious reasons (rats, beetles,
slugs, the corpses of healthy, recently deceased humans). In
Philadelphia in the late 1940s and early 1950s, having an
electric washing machine was not part of the necessary
equipment of a 'decent' life – we had a combination tub/
scrubbing-board/mangle with a handle that one had to turn
in the basement of the building we lived in. Having a television was an almost unthinkable luxury – acquiring one in
1953 made my grandmother the toast of the whole neighbourhood. Now, however, in most parts of Europe and the
United States, both a washing machine and a television
would probably be considered essentials.

A second important point about the necessity which
is at issue here is that it operates and imposes itself, in most
cases, at a very general level, and there is a long path moving
through a large number of steps by which this necessity
eventually articulates itself and fastens itself on some highly
specific task. Perhaps it is true that I need water, and there is
nothing much else that can be said about that: virtually
nothing else is substitutable for it, so the path from the
general statement 'humans need water' to any specific

necessity ('You have been working in the hot sun all day, and need to drink a glass of water') is direct and simple. But many human needs don't have that simple structure. For instance, I also need sufficiently nutritious food (a rule expressing a general necessity), but in any specific case one food can replace another without grave ill effects: instead of rice we could have pasta, or potatoes. Equally it is not necessary that I eat this cauliflower – some broccoli or samphire would do equally well – so, although I must eat something (eventually, or I will suffer for it), I do not with the same absolute and clear necessity need to have a cauliflower or a mango to eat now. Even if I am diabetic I can usually substitute one source of sucrose for another.

Analogously, even if one assumes the goal of continued subsistence, it was not necessary for my father to work at *that* particular job which he had at US Steel. He could have worked at a job different from the one he had in the same mill, or he could have found some similar work in a similar plant (which would probably have required moving), or tried a different kind of work, but it was necessary for him to take *some* job, *one or the other from among those realistically available to him.* He had no inherited wealth, entitlements (stocks or bonds), or other resources (such as my uncle's farm) which would have permitted him to live without engaging in waged labour, and no matter how many jobs as lawyers, carpenters, acrobats, teachers of Spanish, or, for that matter, tool-and-die-makers were 'open', they were not realistically available to him. The same was true of jobs as a railway mechanic in Sweden, Poland, or Italy.

Individual and Social Necessity

A third important point about the necessity of work is that work is 'necessary' in two distinct senses for two different agents or quasi-agents. Work is a necessity for individuals, but it is also a necessity for societies as a whole. I must work if I wish to have food and drink and lead a decent life, but my society as a whole (however that is specified) must also work so that food is grown, drink made available, consumer products produced, and essential services provided, if we are all to survive and lead a minimally acceptable life. That this socially necessary production is absolutely essential for almost any kind of individual work that we know is obvious. My father's work would have been impossible, and would in fact have made no sense at all, in a world without diesel locomotives, railways, and steel mills, none of which he produced himself, and although it is not in the same way inconceivable that my uncle, or someone very like him with appropriate pre-industrial agricultural skills, could have worked his farm without a tractor, in fact he and his family could not have survived without one. The tractor was the product of a mechanised society, which also could have been said to have needed to produce a certain amount of them. It would have made no sense to say of my uncle that he needed to produce a tractor himself because he was about as much capable of doing that on his own (or with the help of his family) as I am of flying to Mars by flapping my arms.

Thus, the need a society has for work to be done and the need each individual has to work are not at all the same thing. In most societies that have existed up to now, as far as we can tell, it would not have been possible for most people to remain completely idle and make no contribution to ensuring the subsistence of the group. If not direct physical necessity, then some combination of that and various forms of social pressure would usually suffice to ensure that anyone who could work would make some kind of contribution to social production and reproduction. Some societies, for instance those of 'really existing socialism' which could be found in Eastern Europe between 1945 and 1989, even had an official policy of insisting that every individual take some part in social production – failure to work was an instance of 'social parasitism' and something in principle punishable by law (often subsumed under legislation against general anti-social behaviour). In most human societies, however, there will be at least a few individuals – some very wealthy, very privileged, or otherwise entitled persons – who will be (in fact, even if not in principle) exempt from the necessity of working, but these will need to be a relatively small number because human labour power is in many societies a scarce resource. Even these wealthy or otherwise privileged individuals will need labour – it is just that it will be the labour of others, without which they would not survive.

The two senses of 'necessity' come apart then. Work is a *social* necessity in that every society (considered as a whole) has certain tasks which 'need to be' performed if the society is to maintain itself in existence. This does not imply that every individual member of that society individually must participate in discharging those tasks. Work is not always necessary for each individual, because those with the right entitlements can be exempt. Without farmers, teamsters, and railways food would not be produced and distributed, and so it is a social necessity that someone do the farming, although it is not necessary for each individual to be a farmer or even occasionally work as a farmer.

The two senses of 'necessity' come apart in the other direction, too. From the fact that individuals need to work to survive and lead a minimally acceptable life, it does not follow that what I do to ensure that I have such a life is actually in all senses socially necessary. First of all, not *all* production is of things that are in any sense necessities. The steel produced in the factory where my father worked was mostly used for cans and containers, and although metal containers are highly useful, not all kinds are strictly necessary. Traditionally, a distinction was made between necessities and luxuries, or perhaps between necessities (food and water), conveniences (washing machines), and then luxuries (Strasbourg geese, opera, calf-leather-bound books, diamonds). The distinction between necessities, conveniences, and luxuries is, of course, almost never sharp, and it is historically constantly changing and highly dependent on the wider social context. Between 1950 and 1980 a washing machine moved from the category of luxury to that of necessity. In a society of mostly small, independent farms, those who work the farms will need some mode of transport for their agricultural produce, such as a horse and wagon in order to get to railheads and then railways; the farmers won't, perhaps, strictly 'need' individual cars. Sometimes, however, a factory is built at a certain distance from any habitation, and no public transport is available, so having a car becomes a necessity for anyone wanting employment there. There is also production of luxury goods which by their very nature are not necessary or even particularly useful. Think about the steel produced in some plants which was specifically made to serve for ornaments on cars, such as the huge tail-fins on some of the US cars manufactured in the 1960s, which were thought by some, even at the time, to be superfluous and wasteful, and which some, in addition, actually found to be aesthetically unappealing, and were only so widely desired because they were so visibly expensive and useless. Finally, lots of people satisfy their need for work by producing objects that are not just useless and socially unnecessary, but actively harmful. The tobacco industry employed thousands of workers for decades.

Money and Credit

Work in my father's world was completely monetarised. 'I need to work' meant 'I need to make a living,' which in turn meant 'I need to make money.' In our societies money is the virtually universal means of acquiring what we need. Perhaps it is not an absolutely universally useful instrument for satisfying absolutely all needs – maybe I need love, self-respect, a sense of meaning in my life, and money will not buy those things – but it certainly is the case that, for a very wide range of other basic needs, in a society like ours money will do the trick. My uncle in Indiana may have originally 'needed' to plough and harvest his field because it contained maize, some of which the members of his family would consume directly and some of which he fed to his farm animals (so that the members of his family could eventually eat them). More and more frequently, however, what he needed was money – to pay his taxes, buy fertiliser for his fields and fuel for his farm vehicles and machines, get medical attention for his livestock and his children when they were unwell, etc. Because the need for money is not as immediate as that for air or water, this does not mean that it is any less real. In a fully monetarised society like ours, the immediate visible form that the 'need to work' takes for most people is a need to acquire money.

Money, no matter how useful, does not stand on its own two feet. When my uncle's house burned down or when he needed to buy a large piece of agricultural machinery, he increasingly came to think of what he needed not as 'money' but as 'credit'. Would the bank advance him the large sum of money he needed (in order to replace his broken combine harvester, so that he could harvest, sell his crop, and use the money to buy food, clothing, and other necessities for his family)? Since the financial crash of 2008 it has become commonplace to think of banks as inherently profligate institutions giving credit almost unthinkingly left and right, with a cavalier attitude toward risk, doing virtually anything to expand the amount they lend. This, however, was historically an aberration, created by a highly specific political policy which massively deregulated the financial sector and created a situation of perverse incentives to particularly irresponsible lending. Before the Big Bang of deregulation, most banks were keen to manage the risk they ran by lending responsibly, that is, only to individuals and enterprises that were 'creditworthy'. One could show oneself to be creditworthy by long years of diligent work, intelligent management, frugality, and punctilious repayment of existing debts. So one way of looking at my uncle's situation is that he had to keep working assiduously to satisfy a need he had to be (seen to be) creditworthy (when the day came that he would require a loan or an advance).

The way in which I have discussed money and creditworthiness might suggest that the realm of credit was something derivative or even parasitic, an appendix hooked on to the monetary system as a kind of afterthought.[1] For various reasons, this is the way things might seem to us, but actually – conceptually and historically – the order ought to be reversed. Credit and creditworthiness are both historically older and logically more fundamental than the monetary system. Even before the invention of money, farmers who lost their crops as a result of natural disasters might beg their more fortunate unaffected neighbours for an advance of seed and provisions, with a promise of return in kind or in the form of labour in their creditors' fields come harvest time. If food and seed were really scarce and precious, it would be natural for those who still had some not to waste it by giving it to people who were notoriously incompetent, idle, or unreliable, or whose promises of compensatory help in the future could not be trusted. This would be a rudimentary assessment of creditworthiness. So one of the reasons I need to work (and to be seen to work) is to maintain my status as minimally creditworthy, because without that, in a precarious world, I run great risks if I am eventually in difficulties. Since the appearance of assiduous application, dutifulness, and sobriety can differ from the reality of these things, there is a gap that can be exploited by the unscrupulous, and for that reason in many societies lenders take special precautions before advancing funds to people whom they have not thoroughly investigated.

The immediate form in which the necessity to work presents itself is that I must work to make money. Money, however, is something that is inherently instrumental; it is the mere tool par excellence. No one can eat cash – money is important only in its use, only for what it can buy. A miser may accumulate money for its own sake, but avarice in the classic sense, the simple hoarding of more and more money which is never used for anything, is just a psychological perversion. The traditional miser, for instance Molière's Harpagon, is very different from a more modern figure who might superficially seem to have some similarities to him, the billionaire 'investor' who desires to accrue money (in the form nowadays of shares, bonds, lines of credit, and other complex instruments) without limit. The difference is that the billionaire seeks more of something not simply to hoard it, but to use ever greater financial leverage to acquire power and control. Simply hoarding things does not in general give one control of anything. Avarice, one could say, belongs to the world of immediate consumption, which is in itself naturally limited: how many kilos of potatoes can one person (and her family and friends) eat? We all know sad cases of people who spend their whole life working and economising and die with – for example – a well-stocked cellar full of the wine they did not drink because they were saving it (or did not even work themselves up to that explicit thought, just followed a hoarding instinct). The miser violates a basic imperative in a simple system of work and consumption, by taking money radically out of circulation. The lust for indefinitely expanding financial power today, which would eventually allow you to buy newspapers, radio stations, and whole shoals of lawyers and politicians, establish research institutes devoted to promoting legislation that favours your interests, bankroll lobbying and public relations campaigns, etc. has no proper name (yet), but it belongs to a different context altogether and, whatever it might be, if it is a perversion, it is one in a different sense from old-style avarice. It is not connected with consumption, but is a form of desire for more and more control, and, as such, a kind of rational reflection of the basic imperatives of our economic system.

Since it must seem to many people that the immediate goal of work is the acquisition of money, and since money is something inherently instrumental which has no value of its own, this can lead to a strong association of work with that which is instrumental. Work, then, can come to seem to be in its very essence something we do not do for its own sake but only for something else which we can use it to acquire. In the technical vocabulary which philosophers have developed, work is always merely a means to an end, never an end in itself.

We have spoken of one perversion of the natural means/ends relation, the vice they called 'avarice'. In the nineteenth century, Marx diagnosed what he took to be another serious perversion of the means–end relation when he discussed the nature of work in the capitalist form of production.[2] The natural state of affairs, Marx thought, was that people worked *in order to live*, that is, they did some strenuous and perhaps slightly disagreeable things in order to be able to live a life full of a variety of different activities:

they cleared out the rubbish from the house, for instance, so that there was an agreeable space for games, study, social interaction, eating. As always with Marx, it is the variety and fluidity of the activities involved and the way in which they were connected with the possible further development of human powers which is most important. The members of the nineteenth-century proletariat, though, rather than working in order to live, were forced to live *in order to work*. That is, they could not develop any of their capacities freely, but *all* activities of their lives had to be ruthlessly subordinated to the single goal of working. Since this was a reversal of the natural teleological relation, it was right to call it a 'perversion'. In the late twentieth century, a similar idea would be taken out of the context of social criticism and transformed into a matter of individual psychology, so that certain people would be called 'workaholics'; such people were thought to have a pathological dependence on what should be an activity that was an important enough part of human life, but that needed to be kept in its place.

Objectivity

The third main element in the concept of work is that there is a product that can be detached from the process of production and evaluated in its own terms, independently of the attitudes and intentions of the person(s) who produced it. The most obvious examples of a product are physical objects: the cobs of maize, bushels of wheat, and watermelons grown and harvested on a farm, or the sheets of steel produced in the steel mill. However, just as 'strenuousness' can first be a property of physical activity but then come to be used of mental or moral exertion, so 'producing a product' can mean not producing a physical object, such as a piece of sheet-metal, but a more abstract process, such as writing a book, composing a piece of music, constructing an argument or theorem, or directing a play.

Goods and Services

Some economists distinguish two kinds of work: producing goods and rendering services. Even directing a play can be seen as the production of a kind of product: there is a performance which takes place at a particular time and can be evaluated. In contrast, rendering a service would be the kind of work done by a physiotherapist, an astrologer, or a person who washes cars. In such cases there may be a change of state (filthy car becomes clean, person unable to bend a leg regains the use of it, person in a state of anxiety about the future becomes confident [even if we would judge that that confidence is misplaced]), but there is no detachable product.

This distinction between goods and services is not sharp. The wig-maker works by making a wig (a 'good'), but the barber works, too, by washing and cutting your hair. A stylist, too, is working by merely arranging what is already there in an attractive way. We may even say that an image-consultant who does no more than just have a series of general conversations with you about aesthetics and soci-ology is working ('This is how they are doing it in *really* fashionable circles now'). This is not, in itself, a denigration of what a stylist or image-consultant might do, and certainly not in itself a reason to think what they do could not count as work.

The fluid and relatively insubstantial nature of the distinction between goods and services, with a gradual transition from one to the other, also emerges in stark relief if one reflects that, in one sense, my father's job belonged to the service sector in that he did not himself through his own direct action contribute to the production of the steel; he did not fire the ore or even himself move it or the resulting iron and steel, in their various forms, from one physical location to another, as the drivers of the locomotive and the operators of the cranes and fork-lifts did. He serviced the engines, inspecting them periodically to maintain them in working order and fixing them when they broke down. What was important was that there was a close, unmistakable, and objective physical connection between what he did, the ability of the locomotives and cranes to function, and the eventual outcome: the huge stacks and coils of sheet steel that were loaded into barges and freight-cars for dispatch elsewhere for use in further industrial processes.

So one might try to construct, by a series of small incremental steps, a sequence starting from my father's case, taking it, for the moment, as a kind of paradigm of work. Suppose that what he is doing is repairing a crane which is broken.

(1) He follows objective procedures – that is, he visibly manipulates parts of the crane in a tangible way, not at random, but following some more or less set rules which

could be formulated and followed equally by any other mechanic, with the result that the crane works again, and through a further series of identifiable mechanical steps, the production process continues and eventually the coils and sheets of steel emerge at the end.

Suppose now that it is not the crane itself that is broken, but the operator who has been slightly hurt; suppose he has cut himself.

(2) The works nurse (or, in more serious cases, the works doctor) will follow objective procedures in cleaning and dressing the wound, and administering an anti-tetanus shot; these procedures can be formulated and are those more or less any doctor or nurse would follow; if all goes well and there are no complications, the crane-operator will eventually be able to work the crane again, with the result that production resumes.

In reality, of course, if the injury was anything other than absolutely trivial and immediately curable, the crane-operator would probably be sent home and replaced with another worker that day. What would happen next would depend on the particular socio-economic regime in place: the crane-operator would go to the infirmary, or be sent home on (paid or unpaid) furlough, or laid off, or even dismissed on account of disability, depending on the specific situation and the legal code. The management would have expected a mechanic to do almost *anything* to repair a crane rather than having it scrapped, because it was an expensive piece of machinery. The crane-operator, on the other hand, was just an individual operative from a potentially large pool of qualified workers, and was not nearly as valuable, and the company certainly would not think it could afford to stop production while he recovered. Let us, however, bracket this bit of knowledge about what might actually occur in practice and simply consider the work situation in relative abstraction.

The third case in the sequence is the physiotherapist who provides a service (which is a form of work) when the crane-operator suffers some kind of muscular damage, or chronic strain:

(3) the physiotherapist manipulates the crane-operator's body in a series of identifiable ways with the result that, if all goes well, he can (eventually) bend and extend his limbs in the required way, with the result that he can rejoin the productive process.

Here one can begin to add services that are less and less directly productive, but still in some way essential to production, such as 'industrial cleaners' (like my uncle) who are not, as one might think, primarily interested in aesthetics, but just in removing possible obstacles to the smooth running of the plant: bits of debris that workers could cut themselves on, spilled liquids that might be inflammable, piles of discarded, spoiled, or defective by-products that might block paths that need to be clear for the fork-lifts to operate. Eventually, after an indeterminate further number of entries into the sequence of services, one might get

(n) at some point in the past some teacher, probably following procedures prescribed in a school curriculum manual, taught my father (more or less), the crane-operator, the nurse, and the physiotherapist to read and calculate, thereby allowing them to acquire the skill of following written instructions for operating and repairing machinery (in the case of the former two) and curing minor physical ailments and injuries to the human body (in the case of the latter two), with the result that mechanised production in a very wide range of contexts could begin in the first place and resume when it was interrupted.

Suppose, however, that the crane-operator has not cut his hand or strained a muscle, but begins to suffer from bouts of depression that prevent him from coming to work or from working efficiently or carefully when he does turn up, and consults a psychotherapist:

$(n + \varepsilon)$ the psychotherapist treats the crane-operator for depression in one of a variety of ways, including prescription of medication, or behavioural therapy or a traditional 'talking cure', so that, if all goes well, he can come to control his depression sufficiently to return to work.

If we continue this imaginary sequence, we might try to add even further steps away from the basic paradigm of direct contribution to immediate production of goods, and eventually come to

(Ω) The priest (minister, imam, rabbi, guru, bonze, Kantian philosopher etc.) gives general religious consolation to workers and their families, tries to explain to them that their lives, despite appearances to the contrary, really do have some sense or meaning, gives them some general orientation for action, and encourages them to be dutiful in their work, thereby, if all goes well, preventing them from committing suicide, or falling prey to terminal lethargy or destructive insouciance; as a result production can continue.

In this progression, each step seems to be located further and further on a scale with several dimensions. The connection between work and result becomes more and more highly mediated by mental, psychological, and attitudinal factors, rather than being a question of a simple mechanical process. Hence the connection is less visible, and easier to fake.

This does not mean that the connection between my father and the motions he makes to fix the crane is without any mental or psychological component. Certainly, if one takes a sufficiently broad view of the context, it was necessary for mechanics minimally to have their wits about them in dealing with whatever the problem was. Still, what a mechanic does to get production going is, in an obvious sense, moving a part of the machinery (for example), whereas what the religious specialist does to get things moving is to perform religious ceremonies and gestures and to speak in such a way that enough members of his or her congregation understand and find themselves motivated to show up, fresh and, even if not exactly bushy-tailed, at least willing to work the next day.

A further component of the idea of objectivity which occurs here is the assumption that if the process is 'objective', the result can be predicted and replicated. The result is not a one-off or an accidental consequence and it does not depend on some magical rapport between a particular individual and the work-process. As one moves through the examples, the procedures used become less easy to formulate, less well codified and routinised, less easy for someone else to replicate (and thus less 'objective').

The Autotelic

Even if one accepts that this kind of step-by-step progression can be constructed, it certainly seems as if something has gone at least slightly wrong if teaching a child to read or consoling the bereaved is construed exclusively as a means to the production of an end; the distortion is compounded if that end is thought necessarily to be the continuation or expansion of production. The idea that I try to regain my health and the use of my limbs *in order to be able to produce coils of steel* again is already slightly bizarre in itself, and to think that this is really the *only* reason I wish to recover would represent a deep-seated kind of alienation. The *non plus ultra* of this form of aberration is described in Heine's poem *Das Sklavenschiff*,[3] where a slaver discovers that too many of the slaves who are immobilised and locked down in the hold of his ship are dying of 'melancholy' during the Middle Passage. So he forces them to come on deck, to sing, dance, and be merry 'because otherwise my business would be ruined'. Here the slaves are forced to satisfy perfectly natural human needs for sunlight, movement, activity, and even play, and to do that *only* in order then to be sold into a life of coerced labour.

Certainly, virtually all traditional philosophers have thought that if you wished to have your psyche in order, simply so that you would then be able to work, you were at the least seriously mistaken and probably deranged. If you had a healthy soul, *one* result would be that you would be able to work, and so in some sense it was not false to say that you wanted to get healthy in order to work; but in a non-perverted state it would also be the case that having your soul minimally in order had value in itself and independently of any further consequence that such health might have. In fact, one might even think that the question 'what is the value of having a healthy soul?' made no sense at all. Psychic health was 'autotelic', an unquestionable end in itself. Some philosophers, Plato's Socrates for instance, might say that the health of one's soul was the most autotelic thing (or state?) that existed for a human being.[4] At least if we look at the world from the point of view of individuals, production does not seem to be the only possible final framework for thinking about life.

2   The Organisation of Work

'Work' in the sense of interest here is a social category. This means that the way work is socially organised is not merely some further external fact about it, but rather is something that needs to be considered in detail. This chapter will have two parts. First, I'll try to say something about how we, nowadays in Western societies, think about the way work is organised, and then I will discuss some existing historical alternatives to this way of thinking about the organisation of work.

In Our World

Jobs

In the previous section I spoke of the two categories into which 'work' is sometimes divided, production of goods and rendering of services, but more precisely, I should probably say that these are the two recognised categories of 'employment'. 'Work' and 'employment' are not the same, although they are related.

There are two social features of work in the modern world which distinguish it from work as it has been performed in many other places and times. First of all, modern work characteristically takes the form of a 'job', which is a highly specific social institution in which an individual performs a particular kind of function repeatedly on a regular basis, often at fixed hours which they do not set themselves and in a separate place. Work in the modern world is not just something you do, even some strenuous necessary activity that you do with a strictly instrumental goal in mind, like cooking, cleaning, or digging the garden. These are all instances of work, and in one sense they are of course jobs, but not in the full and emphatic sense in which that term is used. When a parent tells an adolescent to 'get a job', this is not usually intended to mean 'do some (random and otherwise unspecified) strenuous activity directed at bringing something about in the world', even if what is brought about is something useful or necessary. The adolescent hasn't acquired a job if he or she voluntarily joins a work crew doing something as essential as, say, shoring up the flood defences on an afternoon when the water is rising, or is commandeered by the military to move munitions from one place to another during civil unrest. A job is something I do *regularly*, repeatedly, according to a schedule – the continuous exercise of a social role such as waiting on tables in a restaurant, piloting ships into a harbour, drilling the cavities in people's teeth. People in offices used to work '9 to 5' from Monday to Friday, and the steel mill where my father worked had three shifts (8am to 4pm, 4pm to midnight, and midnight to 8am, seven days a week), and there were highly structured arrangements for starting and finishing the day's work. In many places there was a time clock, and one needed to punch oneself in and out at the beginning and end of the working day; without clocking in one was not paid. The factory system was, after all, about rigorous control of space (the work-place), time (the working day), and motion (both that of material and that of the humans working it). A job, then, is a form of continuous and structured, socially recognised, employment. While work can in principle be thought of almost in purely physical terms, or in physical and moral terms, a job is a social structure and a social creation.

The second feature of work in societies like ours is that, although there are recognised jobs that are unpaid, such as those of the volunteers who work, even full-time, without pay at charity shops, there is a kind of tacit everyday assumption that a proper job will be one for which one is paid. This, as has already been mentioned, is one reason why things like housework and childcare, which are clearly both strenuous and necessary, and have outcomes as objective as anything could be, are not considered proper jobs. As forms of activity they don't have the right structure; they don't fall into the appropriate discrete packets of activity: the activity of keeping a house in order or taking care of a child is *never* done; it has no discrete beginning or end, and it does not require moving to a separate designated work-space. Finally, in the overwhelming majority of cases these activities are not remunerated, except in the case of a very few professionals who specifically *make* them into 'jobs' (such as nannies or cooks).

It is not only that in our societies work is considered in the first instance to be divided into structured jobs, but these are also put in a roughly hierarchical order which ranks types of regular, fixed employment: there are (mere) jobs, careers, professions, and vocations. This is a hierarchy of status or prestige, but also one that expresses itself even in the language we use to speak of the remuneration each kind of employment generally attracts: a person who has a job gets pay or wages; someone with a career receives a salary, and those higher up the scale get stipends, honoraria, and retainers. Since this is an important feature of work as we know it, it might make sense to think about this structure for a moment.

Given that we are talking in this section about structured employment rather than work in general, let us put aside the categories of people who clearly do strenuous, necessary activity, but do not fit into the schema. They are, first of all, people (mostly women) who work extremely hard without remuneration at housework, childcare, tending of the elderly, and similar 'domestic' tasks, and then, to the extent to which they still exist, genuinely subsistence farmers, hunters, pastoralists, who live on what they raise, tend, or catch, and finally the various sorts of serfs and other dependent labourers who are perhaps in some way remunerated, but not with money. These groups are outside the system and will have to be considered separately. Also in a sense outside the system are proper slaves, who are below the bottom of the hierarchy.

Slaves, serfs, and other dependent labourers are clearly an important group in the world economy as a whole, and can be found even in advanced economies in which their existence might not be formally recognised or may be strictly illegal. We tend not to 'see' slaves, and we are used to thinking in particular that there is no slavery in the modern world, except in various metaphorical senses (wage-slavery, a slave to his passions), but, of course, numerous reports have shown that this is not the case. The sex industries everywhere are full of women who are enslaved (even if one uses that term in the strictest possible sense), and gangs of serfs and other dependent labourers are frequently used in agriculture everywhere in Europe. These become visible only rarely, such as when a group of Chinese forced labourers drowned in Morecambe Bay in the UK a few years ago, but reliable reports indicate that they are just the tip of the iceberg.

There is no doubt but that the slave works. In some societies at some times, for instance in ancient Rome, there might have been a mere handful of slaves who were there just for show, to increase their masters' prestige, while the rest worked at more strenuous jobs, but nowadays working is what a slave is there for, in fact is virtually all they are there for. Slaves, too, by definition, may get rations to keep them alive and able to work, but they get no remuneration of any kind, no pay. Slaves work and they may have occupations (cook, field-hand, groom, or, in the ancient world, policeman, doctor, or miner) or functions, but they are not in (or out of) employment, and they do not in the full sense have a job. Slaves are at the bottom of the pecking order of fixed employment. No fixed working conditions and no pay. Nothing.

Just above slavery with, as it were, its fingers just barely grasping the bottom rung of the employment ladder, is oddjobbing, casual day-labour, or what used to be called 'temping'. This describes a person who has some kind of separate, paid employment at least some of the time, but whose work has no continuity at all, and whose employment is insecure even in the short term. Pay is calculated and calibrated by days or even by hours, and is often disbursed at the end of each working day. The most disadvantaged of this group are those on 'zero hours' contracts. Such workers are paid only for the hours they actually work, but are not guaranteed any number of hours of work per week. In addition, many must keep themselves on call to work at any time of the employer's choice. So not only do they not know what they will be paid in any given day, they also cannot try to find other employment that would interfere with their availability.

A proper or regular job is thus a separate activity with relatively fixed hours and working conditions, usually in a separate location, with fixed, reliable remuneration, measured in months or years, rather days or weeks. It is employment that one can be expected to keep for a reasonable period of time. One receives for it not just a payment, but wages.

Careers and Professions

Further up the hierarchy there stands a career. To have a career suggests that I do what I do for remuneration, but that the job in question is in principle something for the long term. Usually there is also an implication that the career has some specific entry conditions connected with skill in some kind of performance, that it requires some training, and that it has some kind of internal structure of advancement. Furthermore, there is often some idea that the person who has the career has an attitude of at least minimal commitment toward that employment, a non-superficial engagement with it, and thus that it plays a certain role in the life of the person who embarks on it.

On the next rung of the hierarchical ladder we find professions, which are careers of a particular kind. Archetypical professions are accountancy, medicine, architecture, engineering, law. Just as a job is not just a random collection of acts of work, but a social role devoted to performing certain tasks, so a profession is not just a job or a career, but one which is thought to require a particularly high level of specialised skills, qualifications, and training, and the exercise of which is thought to be subject to a special code of practice, which is (ideally) enforced by an organised body of the practitioners of the profession. It is not that all jobs that are not professions are unskilled; my father was very proud of the fact that he 'had his papers' (certificates of successful completion of his two-year apprenticeship as a locomotive mechanic) and was *not* an 'unskilled labourer', and my mother had attended secretarial college to learn typing and shorthand to a high level, but being a mechanic was a job and being a secretary a career not a profession. Part of the difference in this classification was that being a mechanic was a 'blue-collar' job – in fact my father's hands were almost always covered with industrial grease – whereas being a secretary was 'white-collar' – working in an office, not shop or a mill. I think that some assumptions about gender were being expressed in that it was absolutely routinely expected that a man had to have a job, whereas for a woman marriage and domestic work were expected, and so training as a secretary (and continuing to work) was a violation of expectations and thus required more commitment on the part of someone who did it.

The German sociologist Max Weber analysed what he thought was the pervasive tendency in the modern world toward what he called 'bureaucratisation',[1] that is toward imposing on all activities an organisational structure in which there is a series of superimposed groups, the higher-ranking ones purportedly having more training, experience, and competence than the lower-ranked ones, and in which those higher on the scale had more authority. One can then (and is in some sense expected to) rise through the ranks or attain positions of greater authority and responsibility through the exercise of the profession. This bureaucratic model is endemic in modern professions. It is as if the hierarchical ranking of forms of employment were reproduced here *within* a particular profession. At each stage, greater knowledge and experience is supposed to give access to the next step up and greater responsibility and authority.

My father, despite his 'papers', would not have been considered to have a profession, probably because the skills he had been trained to exercise were considered to be binary: the assumption was that there were a few well-defined types of problematic situations which he was trained to recognise, and a few solutions he had learned. There was little sense that *his* skill could be better or less well exercised. Any trained mechanic would know the solution; someone without training would not. If things got hopeless, the final recourse was not to a higher-grade mechanic (which didn't exist), but to 'the engineers' ('the men with the slide-rules', my father would say). Engineering *is*, of course, a recognised profession, and its practitioners were supposed, by virtue of their professional training, to have skills that were unlike my father's in that they were thought to be indefinitely expandable and applicable, and to include an open-ended ability to confront and deal with unexpected situations, and invent new solutions. One might say that there was some element of creativity in the characteristic task of the engineer which was presumed to be absent in the work of the mechanic, and that that was part of the reason why the engineer had a profession and my father had a job.

Partly, of course, the separation between mechanics and engineers was an ideological fiction. No competent mechanic merely followed routine procedures, such as those in the service manuals, and virtually all mechanics also develop their own non-standard, but perfectly effective, ways of doing things. They were also perfectly capable of dealing with new difficulties that turned up, but were not discussed in the manuals. On the other hand, it would not be surprising if there was an element of socially constructed reality to the contrast. What capacities workers will develop, including ingenuity and initiative, in part depends on how they trained, what expectations people have about them, and the actual conditions under which they work, and if the mechanics are encouraged to call in the engineers at the drop of a hat, that will certainly not encourage them to develop their problem-solving capacities.

The call for the engineers indicates something else about the way some work in the modern world is organised. In my father's view the hierarchy of the factory in which he worked was clear: labourers (completely unskilled people who did the simplest manual labour), men (simple workers like him), foremen (former simple workers who had been promoted to positions of local authority), supervisors; then an unbridgeable gap, above which came engineers; then a further unbridgeable gap above which came management; and at the very top, out of sight, 'Pittsburgh' (site of the corporate headquarters of US Steel). I note then that this is a clear hierarchy, but it is not a professional hierarchy. The managers were *not* even more highly qualified engineers (although some of them may have started their working lives as engineers). Rather it was a hierarchy of authority, that is, of power to command. A beginning junior doctor is doing the same kind of thing as a senior consultant, although perhaps treating mainly simpler and more straightforward cases, but no manager did anything at all comparable to what an actual worker did. What was true was not that the manager could fix the broken pump better than the engineer or the worker, but that the manager could give the engineer and the worker orders.

Professions are often governed by special codes of practice which go beyond what is legally required of all those subject to the laws in question, and also sometimes beyond what is morally expected of everyone. Since the practice of archetypical professions, such as medicine, is thought to require a certain autonomy of judgement, such professions are also permitted a high level of self-regulation. The idea is that not everyone can type, but almost anyone can judge who is a good typist – speed and lack of errors – whereas on the other hand, only someone with medical training can really judge how good someone is as a doctor. This is not because it is always difficult to judge the outcomes – whether a patient dies or not is as visible to an outsider as the number of errors a typist makes – but because it is hard for a lay person to judge how difficult, obscure, and problematic it is to diagnose and treat given cases. That lots of patients who have Ebola die is not necessarily a sign that the doctor in charge is incompetent.

Since a profession requires a long and complex training and has an associated code of ethics, it will be likely to impinge to a great extent on a practitioner's life and to impress its ethos on it. The connection of the individual with the employment is, therefore, thought to be greater in the case of a profession: a secretary may change his or her job and start a career as a cook (or vice versa), but (at least in principle) once a doctor, always a doctor. In addition, for the grammarian, it was said (taking 'being a grammarian' as a kind of stand-in for any profession) 'all reality is grammatical', but my mother never suffered from the delusion of thinking that all reality was secretarial. On the other hand, because professions are construed to be self-regulating and to require the exercise of independent judgement, there is a general sense that there is more freedom and more room for at least limited self-expression in a profession than in some other jobs.

Vocations

Finally, there is the idea of an occupation which is not (only) a job, career, or profession but a vocation. The idea of a vocation clearly has its origins in religious thought:

God – a powerful cosmic force with moral standing that is construed as being fully *outside* the individual in question – was thought to 'call', to predispose, to invite, or to order imperatively some individual to lead some specific kind of highly structured life. It would seem natural, if I am trying to decide what to do in life, to give weight to factors that relate primarily to myself. What can I do? What properties do I have? What abilities and skills? Also what deficiencies and weaknesses? For which among the available options of employment am I maximally (or at all) suited? I will also consider my own preferences. What do I want to do? People in our society are strongly encouraged to do what they are considered to have a natural aptitude for, and therefore it is advantageous also to want (very strongly) to do what you are good at, thereby coordinating the two dimensions. However, most people will be familiar with cases in which there is a striking discrepancy between what someone desperately wishes to do and what he or she is capable of. There is the virtually tone-deaf person who insists on continuing to play an instrument (badly), but also the exceptionally gifted footballer, chess-player, or cook who hates and avoids doing what they are actually supremely good at, and tries to do something else with disastrous results. Other examples include the wonderful comic actor who is dreadful in tragic roles but insists on playing them, the novelist who dreams (in vain) of being a successful playwright, or the various celebrities who have failed as fashion designers.

The whole idea of a 'vocation' taken strictly is an archaic survival, despite Max Weber's insistence on the importance it originally played in the genesis of our modern

46

world of work. In a way, having at one's disposal the idea of a 'vocation' takes the pressure off the decision process by taking it out of the individual's hands. If the god tells you to do something, you refuse at your peril. This does not, of course, mean that individuals do not in fact struggle against accepting vocations that are contrary to what they think they want. Lots of prophets make it clear that they would rather not be a god's mouthpiece. After all, being a prophet was by no means always a cushy job: many of them ended up reviled; many were persecuted, or consigned to sit on a dungheap, scratching their scabs with a broken potsherd, or even crucified. Given this, the unwillingness of the potential prophet to accept his calling is a recurrent dramatic theme in religious literature. Probably the most famous treatment of this topic in literature is Vergil's epic about a man forced by the gods to spend his life doing what he would rather not: *Italiam non sponte sequor* ('It is not that I *want* to go to Italy') Aeneas says (*Aeneid*, IV.361), but an even more powerful and incisive exploration of this theme is in Schönberg's opera *Moses und Aron*, where Moses is not only unwilling, but distinctly unsuited to the role of enunciating the word of the Lord, because he has a speech impediment. Here the fact that the vocation is precisely the opposite of anything that could be thought to be grounded either in natural ability or in individual desire seems almost intended to add objectivity and credibility to the calling, to indicate that it really *must* come from a source other than the subject's own preferences. One may struggle against such a vocation, but such a struggle makes sense only if the person called admits that the thing he or she is called to has inherent, objective importance. A career is something for which one makes a place in one's life, and even a profession exercised over a lifetime leaves room for other things – it was said that Vienna at the turn of the nineteenth–twentieth century had the very best doctors' string quartets in the world – but a vocation is something which permeates and takes over all of life. The discharge of the vocation is supposed to be an end in itself, requiring full commitment. Correspondingly, there is a distinct terminology used for the remuneration of those pursuing a vocation. My cousin, who was a Roman Catholic priest, would have received a 'stipend', and the relation of this remuneration to the work he did was also supposed to be contingent. Since he was assumed to have a vocation (or, as Protestants would put it, a 'calling'), this meant that he would be doing his job for life. There was a recognition that priests could become disabled, for instance by virtue of becoming visibly senile and unable to perform their functions, and provision was made for such people, but there was no concept of 'retirement'. Furthermore, my cousin was assumed to be doing all that he did *ad maiorem Dei gloriam* ('for the greater glory of God' – that is, for its own sake) and certainly not for any financial (or other temporal) rewards, so the money he received was not calculated to be for specific services rendered; rather, it was directed, as it were, to his life as a whole. It was something to enable his continued physical existence as a mere precondition to his continuance in his priestly function. He performed services – like weddings, baptisms and funerals – for which specific monetary payments were expected, but they were usually called

48

something like 'donations', and went not directly to him but to the parish with which he was associated.

The idea of a vocation makes perfect sense if there is a god or gods or some such thing as Fate or Destiny to ground it, but without that assumption it is very difficult to make sense of the idea that there is something one 'ought' to do which is in principle completely independent of what powers one has and what one wants to do with those powers (or with one's life as a whole). For a while such things as family tradition may take the place of destiny, but these tend to lose their force in a society based on individual free choice. When the idea of a calling or vocation is secularised, it is reduced to meaning simply that a person has unique gifts that cannot be acquired just by volition, hard work, or training and that make him or her particularly suited to performing some task at an especially high level of success. One hears people say that it would be a 'waste' not to use the skills in question. Sometimes this means 'we the potential audience would really like to hear the playing of a violinist who is *that* good', but sometimes the concern seems more disinterested, depending on the quasi-Leibnizian ontological assumption that skills are there to be used. Why make this ontological assumption?[2] It is hard to see how it could reasonably have survived the end of natural teleology, but I think that many people in our society continued to make it until very recently, when intensely individualist attitudes, exclusively focused on the individual's actual desires, began to undermine it.

In the modern secularised version, a special emphasis comes also to be put on the psychological attitudes and the full commitment of the person who has the calling. The question is not 'What am I called to do?' but 'What do I (really) want to do?,' and that is often accompanied by the further question 'Of what level of commitment am I capable?,' so the psychoanalyst (and perhaps also the trainer or coach) takes the place of the priest and theologian as shaper of aspiration and vocational counsellor.

Finally, the religious origin of the idea of a 'vocation' is probably also responsible for the sense we have that the term cannot be used for just *any* form of work, job, or profession, but ideally only for those whose goal can be seen not only as generally good or useful, but as in some way sublime, such as curing the sick, expanding human horizons, protecting the weak, teaching the young, inspiring future generations. It seems to us to be a stretch to call house-cleaning a vocation, even though there is no doubt but that it is useful, and some people are better at it than others. Probably it is not considered a possible vocation partly because it is a manual job, especially one associated with women, and thus has low status. Still, no one would say that someone had a vocation to buy and sell things – which is not a manual job – even though certain people might do that assiduously and well.

One important thing that all of these examples of the different ways in which our working life can be structured (into jobs, careers, professions, vocations) show is the deep connection between our economic system and the control of time, and also the close connection between the control of time and the existence of relations of trust between humans (as expressed, for instance, in the decision that a certain person is 'creditworthy'). Nietzsche discusses the way in which, in making a promise, I am claiming that I can control time and myself. 'I will do X tomorrow' means 'Even if my circumstances change and I don't really feel like it, I will make myself do X tomorrow,' and he specifically makes the connection with debt.[3] Being able to run up a debt depends on being able to make someone else trust that you will repay it. Incurring debt is, in general, a way of losing control of one's time because one will have to work to repay the debt.[4]

Trust is also important on the part of employees at the beginning of a work-contract, too. If I take a job, I generally trust that you will pay me – at the end of the day, the end of the week, the end of the month, or the end of the year. How long I can be expected to wait for pay (or for my wages, salary, stipend, or honorarium) is an indication of social expectations about how urgently a typical person doing that kind of job will need the money. People in jobs with lower prestige are expected to live hand-to-mouth and need money; people in higher-status jobs are expected to have access to other resources.

How remuneration is calculated and paid out is of great importance. The reason for this is that, in a society like ours, the longer the period of time for which one can reasonably calculate income and expenses, the better off (in general) one is. This is clear even in everyday life: if I need money by the end of the day in order to feed myself and my family, I am in a much worse position than that of someone who needs to maintain a level of investment and returns during a given decade to keep up the family fortune.

This usually gives employers a positional advantage over their workers in most negotiations. In a similar vein, economic depressions are very bad news for the poor, but can be very good for the wealthy. Established millionaires in the United States, unless they had made spectacularly bad investment decisions, fared very well indeed in the Great Depression of the late 1920s and 1930s. They could look on with equanimity as their income and the market value of their holdings decreased with deflation – since they had more than they absolutely needed even after the fall of the market – *and* they could afford to wait until they could acquire new, viable assets that were suddenly available for purchase because of the fall in their market value. This was a crisis for the poor, but an opportunity for the rich.

Other Ways of Doing Things

The schema presented in the last section did not, of course, treat all forms of work which we think exist in our society or even all forms of employment, but merely gave a bare-bones account of some of the major categories. Obviously there are forms of work that do not easily fit into the schema, such as the work of small independent practitioners of crafts. What, too, of a person who inherits a large sum of money from ancestors (or, for that matter, is able to borrow it) and is actively investing it? Negotiating financial conditions and pursuing a variety of different investment strategies would seem to fit into some features of the schema proposed for work: it can be, I suppose, as psychologically taxing and strenuous as many things that are called 'work' and it requires some concentration, knowledge, and perhaps some judgement. However, it doesn't seem exactly right to call it either a job or a career, and it certainly isn't a 'profession'. People with a vested interest in seeing our regime of work in a particular way may wish to emphasise the role of individual investors and entrepreneurs in the economy more than my schema seems to permit. However that might be, in this section I would like to turn attention away from our own society to some other ways in which work has been organised in other human societies. I make no attempt to give a general overview of *all* the ways in which that has been done. Is this small group of tribal adolescents with their animals just enjoying themselves or are they 'herding'? Was the priest who conducted a ceremony on top of the Sialk ziggurat in the third millennium BC working? This may throw light on some less exotic cases. Thus, the Catholic priest in my school, who gave a certain number of us extra Russian lessons on Saturday mornings, must have received some stipend, although he lived in the *clausura* of the school and took his meals there. But he was paid whatever he was paid for teaching Latin and earned no supplementary income from these activities; he was simply a man who loved teaching languages. So was he working on Saturdays? There is nothing inherently wrong with the indeterminacy of concepts relating to work; that is just the way concepts are, and we live with this fact in our everyday life perfectly comfortably – we just have to learn to recognise and admit this. So in what follows I will discuss simply some striking other forms that the organisation of work has taken, and which I think are for one reason or another particularly relevant.

The kinds of work I shall now discuss have all actually existed, as far as I am aware, at some time and in some place, so there cannot be much question about their possibility, if one poses that question abstractly. Of course, there can be questions about whether they are (still) possible *for us*. To say that another way of working would be possible '*for us*' usually means that we could adopt it *without too much change to other aspects of our social relations and without a radical diminution of our productive capacities and current levels of consumption*. The tacit assumption made here is that people will not voluntarily accept a significant reduction in the standard of consumption to which they have become accustomed. The answer one will get to the question of what is possible for us depends partly on which social relations and what level of productive power we keep constant in assessing the counterfactual, and what is the maximum diminution of our production that we would (or could) accept. These are all deeply political questions.

The Non-existence of Autarchy

Let me start, however, not with the description of a real historical possibility, but with a misleading non-possibility, something which in the relevant sense does not exist, and has never existed, and which yet constitutes a continual ideological temptation for people in our society. What does not exist is completely autarchic individual work. I mean by this the idea of an individual working completely outside society in isolation to satisfy his or her needs, and then by extension, and subsequently, coming together with other similar individuals in various relations of regulated exchange to form society. To say that logically there must have been some individual or some family group who were the first to work may or may not be correct – I think that assertion is too vague to count as potentially true or false – but it is in any case irrelevant. Certainly, as far back as we can trace anything like human work, it is a collective activity pursued in a familial and social context. We move from groups of apes to groups of people; where one wants to place the boundary between these two is mostly a matter of definition. What is certain, though, is that anything like 'individuation' is, before the nineteenth century, a distinctly subordinate and derivative phenomenon.

There is, of course, the phenomenon of subsistence agriculture such as that practised in many traditional peasant societies or that which my uncle in southern Indiana tried (without much success) to practise in the late 1940s and early 1950s, but real subsistence agriculture is completely different from the fantasy of autarchic work. The fantasy is that I (or 'we', the members of my extended family) consume and use *only what we grow or make ourselves*. This was never the case for my uncle, and would not have been conceivable to him. 'Subsistence' for him meant that he did not have to get paid non-agricultural employment (i.e. a paid job off the farm in town) in order to make a living and allow his family to survive. For a brief period he was able to avoid taking paid non-agricultural employment, but only by dint of selling his surplus on the market. This was basically because he could not run the farm without machines that needed fuel, which had to be bought for cash (or credit), because he had some unavoidable other expenses that required cash, such as paying taxes, and finally because his culturally structured expectations about what making a minimally acceptable living meant included such things as sending his numerous children to school and getting them medical attention when they were ill. There may once have been a time when the doctor was remunerated by giving him a chicken, or children were taught to read and write by scratching on pot shards or random bits of broken slate, but by 1950 in southern Indiana those times already belonged to a mythic, or at any rate obsolete, past. Without his machines (and the fuel for them) my uncle's family would have starved within two years, because they did not have the skill needed to cultivate enough of their fields sufficiently efficiently by hand to produce enough to live. And with the machines they were continually dependent on the cash-nexus and the market price. Even Robinson Crusoe, who is one of the earliest and most fully realised literary expressions of the autarchic fantasy, has in fact at his disposal the wreck of a fully equipped ship, from which he salvages some of the very durable, and in some cases actually rather sophisticated, instruments (muskets, a sextant, a watch) which it contained. This is what permits him to survive; so his autarchic life is in fact conducted at the far end of a kind of infinitely long hospital drip that connects him to Europe. The drip is cut at a certain point by shipwreck, but there was enough still flowing in the tube to maintain Crusoe for years.

In fact, rather than being less dependent on 'society', my uncle seemed to me more dependent than my father was. Both the brothers were fully entangled in the money economy by virtue of having credit arrangements with banks for mortgages on houses and cars, but in addition my uncle had loans or credit for lots of machinery, and he was constantly soliciting help in the form of seasonal work from friends, neighbours, and members of the (very extended – my father had eight siblings) family. He seemed always to need a hand for some task or other, no matter what the season. In fairness, I think he reciprocated by lending his children's labour to neighbours from time to time when that was necessary, but, as we know from other sources, borrowed labour, like other things that are borrowed in pre-industrial society, was never very quickly, and never too exactly, returned. My parents had a horror of being in debt, because they took it as a sign of being out of control and potentially in someone else's power, but that is a very post-Puritan Protestant attitude which by this time had come to exert a strong influence even on some Catholic families like mine, but by no means on all. My uncle, for instance, distinguished sharply between being in debt to a *bank* (horrid) and being in debt to neighbours (perfectly normal). Also it was an attitude focused on specifically monetary debt, not the myriad other forms of indebtedness that structure all human societies. My uncle rather tended to act as people in other and older forms of agrarian societies did, and to *prefer* to be in debt (or to have other people in his debt). This reinforced social bonds, after all, and so his reciprocity was never exactly calculated, and no one seemed to be keeping an exact score about it.[5] This was perhaps a pale, slightly decadent reflection of the 'mutual aid' which certain anarchists, such as Kropotkin, have thought was the real basis of human society. Whatever else it was, then, my uncle's work was anything but solitary and pre-social, even if one counts his family as part of him.

Perhaps the example of someone trying to live by selling the produce of a farm in the middle of a fully mon-etarised and industrial society is not a good model of the kind of subsistence agriculture which took place for millennia before money was invented, and which generated at best only modest surpluses. Real subsistence agriculture, one might claim, does not exist when it is possible to produce a large surplus of crop, and it exists only when the money-nexus is absent except perhaps in a rudimentary or marginal form. This, of course, does not mean that true subsistence agricul-tural is autarchically individual; subsistence farmers are com-pletely dependent on social relations, particularly forms of mutual aid, with other farmers, and often with some crafts-men, which can also easily exist outside a cash nexus.

Although the kind of subsistence regime which immediately occurs to us is one based on farming, in fact there have been at least three different historical forms which it has taken.

In the eighteenth century, several thinkers of the Scottish Enlightenment (including Dugald Stewart, Adam Smith, Adam Ferguson, and John Millar) developed theories of history based on a division of types of society. They distinguished four such types, each based on a particular characteristic kind of work which ensured their subsistence:

1. Hunting and gathering
2. Pastoralism
3. Agriculture
4. Commerce

These theoreticians thought that this sequence was universal and invariable. Nowadays it is usually called simply the 'four-stages view' of the development of human society. In the later part of the nineteenth century, a version of this view became dominant which substituted 'industry' for 'commerce' as the fourth stage. If one adds to this the view that human societies only generally become sedentary when they begin to practise agriculture, and the identification of agriculture with large-scale monocrop cultivation of one of the four classic grains – wheat, barley, rice, and maize – then one gets something like the view that still lurks in the back of the mind of most of us who are not professional prehistorians. Recent research suggests that the development of agriculture is immensely more complicated than this image suggests, that the first three stages of the model coexist and overlap much more than the tidy fourfold scheme of successive steps, and that sedentarism long antedates the domestication of the four classic grains. It is clear that for millennia some groups practised a mixture of the first three means of subsistence without any one of them being clearly and inflexibly dominant.[6]

Hunting and Gathering

With these qualifications in place, we turn first to so-called 'hunting-and-gathering' (or 'hunting-and-foraging') modes of subsistence, which must have been the dominant form of human life before the advent of full-scale monolithic agriculture. People engaged in hunting and gathering do not cultivate crops, certainly not systematically, but rather live off the wild foodstuffs they can find and collect from the surrounding environment (berries, locusts and grubs, mushrooms, honey, plants and tubers of various kinds) or from the fish and molluscs they can catch in rivers, lakes, or seas, or from the wild animals they can hunt down. Available resources and game tend to be limited and seasonal, and thus can be exhausted if the band is too big or stays in the same place too long, so it is not surprising that many hunter–gatherers are highly mobile, if not fully nomadic. They move on when, through depletion, food becomes too difficult to obtain in a certain area, although they might eventually return after enough time has passed for the flora and fauna to recover. This in turn means that the possibility of accumulating any surplus is very limited indeed, and there is little incentive to hoard: foraged food or prey that has been hunted down goes bad eventually, so why, especially if you need to respond rapidly to the requirements of a new hunt, burden yourself with a bit of the carcass of last week's kill, which will be rotten in a day or so anyway, especially if there is more fresh game in the next valley? This establishes the characteristic binary rhythm of time in societies in which this mode of sustenance is dominant. There is feast (when the hunters are successful in bringing down a large animal, which must be consumed more or less immediately because there is no way to preserve it), or famine (when the hunters return empty-handed). Under these circumstances it would not be surprising if the people who depended on hunting and foraging had in general a very keen sense of their dependence on natural processes over which they have no control, and also a sense of the balance that would need to exist between human efforts and the regenerative powers of nature, and there is evidence that many such groups are fully aware of this. If you eat most of some kind of vegetation, it may well grow back again next year, but if you exterminate the edible animal life in a region, it may take several years for it to recover, and a human group absolutely dependent, even in part, on hunting will be likely to notice this. Or at any rate the human groups that survived successfully over decades or centuries are likely to have noticed and acted on this observation.

Some regions of the world, though, are particularly endowed with a more or less constant supply of varied animal food. This seems to have been true of southern Mesopotamia 6,000 or 7,000 years ago, when what is now desert was a series of highly fertile wetlands, and this was an important factor in the genesis of the establishment of early settlements there of people exploiting all the food resources available in an area where marsh, dry land, fresh water, and salt water came together.[7]

So is hunting and foraging 'work' for members of these societies? It is certainly true that they perform strenuous, organised activities that are necessary for them to continue to live, and some of these activities exhibit a very high degree of detachable objectivity, but although work does, then, it would seem, exist among groups like this, it is not at all so clear that one can say that anyone has a job. Part of our idea of a job is that X does one thing and Y something else in a systematic way. One of my uncles worked in a car factory; another was a baker; a third sold beauty products. This is division of labour. In hunting-and-gathering societies this division into jobs does not exist in anything like this form. Perhaps the men do one thing (hunt seals) and the women something else (ice-fishing), or perhaps the young and the older and more experienced people do something slightly different, or finally perhaps different clans have slightly different areas of activity, but these will be connected to kinship groups, not individuals. Obviously, too, in hunting-and-foraging societies there will be no such thing as remuneration, although in many groups larger animals which are successfully hunted down will be divided among the hunters and the members of the hunters' extended families according to complicated rules, including kinship rules. These rules will bear almost no relation to anything we would naturally find plausible as remuneration for a job well done, and perhaps that very fact should motivate us to reflect on the oddity and arbitrariness of the rules in our own society that govern the remuneration of work.

Equally, in hunting-and-foraging societies there seems to be little clear sense of a sharp separation between home and a workplace, nor obviously any notion of regular hours of employment. If people are hungry and the game is in sight, off the hunters will go, but people may laze around for a day or two or even three before feeling the need to bestir themselves again. There may be seasonal differences in the kind of activity performed, but this will not, as it were, trickle down to the microstructure of the day. Any distinction there might be between the encampment (where people cook, eat, and sleep) and the bush (where food is collected and game hunted) will be highly relative and contextual in a way it is not generally with us.

Given the reported extreme egalitarianism of social relations in many hunting-and-gathering groups, the 'necessity' to which work is a response will be differently configured from the way it is in our societies and is likely to be very differently experienced. It is one thing to go out to collect locusts or hunt a deer when one begins to feel hungry, and another to go to work to make money to pay the bank for a mortgage which is due on the first day of every month for years. Until the 1960s there was a general assumption that people practising hunting and foraging as their main mode of subsistence were poor and hungry, and that their life was a constant exhausting struggle with the grim necessities of existence. Life in these societies was assumed to conform to Hobbes' assertion about human life before civil society was established: it was 'solitary, poor, nasty, brutish, and short'.[8] Marshall Sahlins argued against this assumption and in favour of the claim that hunter–gatherer societies were, to use his phrase, 'the original affluent societies'.[9] They were not, of course, affluent in the sense that people in them had many possessions, quite the contrary is true, but the members of such societies were well fed and had a very varied diet. They were certainly better fed than most normal members of sedentary agricultural societies. They were also rich in the most important human asset: time and control over one's own time. People in these societies on the whole seemed to satisfy their needs by working much *less* than they do in agricultural societies or even in modern industrial societies; they had more leisure time, and they had much more control than people in other forms of society have over the structuring and the use of their time. Sahlin's thesis is not without its critics, but there seems to be something like a consensus on the basic point he was trying to make.

Pastoralism

A second kind of subsistence regime is one based on pastoralism: the herding and tending of domesticated animals such as sheep, goats, cows, camels, and llamas. Tending animals is perhaps a less strenuous way of providing for the necessities than certain kinds of hunting, for instance the 'persistence-hunting' still practised today by certain bushmen in the Kalahari, which requires the hunters to pursue the prey relentlessly for hours at a time, in the midday sun, in order to exhaust it completely. It is not an accident that the literary model of a relaxed 'idyllic' life in the West is the pastorale: the shepherd idly playing his pipes in Arcadia while languidly surveying his grazing goats and sheep, and exchanging the odd lustful glance with a shepherdess (or, in the case of Vergil [*Eclogue* II], with another shepherd). Is the shepherd really 'working'?

This literary image, derived from Theocritus, Vergil, and their innumerable literary imitators down the centuries, gives at best a highly distorted view of the realities of the raising and herding of livestock as a way of life. Anyone familiar with these realities would find it hard to deny that what herders do is work: they are exerting themselves strenuously in order to obtain the necessities of life, and their activity is much more regular, systematic, and ordered than that of most hunter–gatherers. Cows, I am told, need to be milked at more or less the same time each day, which is one of the reasons why farmers always object to daylight-saving time. One can't just chase a gazelle with one's cousin for six hours one day and then rest in the shade for the next four days. Furthermore, pastoralism seems amply to satisfy the condition of objectivity. The shepherd who goes out in the morning with twenty sheep either comes back with twenty or has lost one (to thieves, wild animals, falls from precipices, simple ovine disorientation); the goats produce one bucket of milk a day or more (or less).

Overgrazing is at least as great a problem for pas-toralists as depletion of animals by excessive hunting is for hunters, but the basic ideology of pastoral societies does not seem to be so much one of balance or equilibrium as of (natural) increase. Pure hunters have no place in their life for accumulated 'wealth', for more than they really need – where would they carry it? Pastoralists, however, can become rich: they can have wealth on the hoof. They don't carry their riches around with them in a bag: it follows them, or is driven before them. So for them it is possible to accumulate a surplus.

So there seems to be no reason to deny that animal husbandry is work, but the activities that give this way of sustaining a family or a group its specific character do seem to be rather different from those familiar to us from the industrial labour which we still use as our model of work. To put it bluntly, the shepherd 'takes care' of or 'cares for' his sheep, rather than just manipulating it like some object, or a machine (or shooting poisoned arrows at it like a hunter). This point is put very clearly by Plato's Socrates in the first book of his *Republic*, when he says that the shepherd tries to foster the well-being, the good of the sheep. The later Christian image of the Good Shepherd laying down his own life for his sheep is a development of this thought, although probably not derived from Plato, and it shows that it is one that was widely shared and not just a Greek eccentricity. My father was, and was strongly encouraged to be, careful in his use of materials and in the way he treated the machines he serviced and repaired, but no one would be likely to say that his job was to foster the well-being of the locomotives and cranes. Perhaps it is just an accident of language that we don't find it natural to use expressions like that, but whether or not that is the case, there is a deep-seated intuition here that will not simply go away. I take no account whatever of the well-being of the chickpeas when I ruthlessly crush them to make *hummous*. The sheep, in contrast, as an animal, is conceived as having some (inherent) welfare that a human might ignore or thwart, but which a shepherd might, could, or should take account of; a piece of metal, though, does not have a state of welfare. It may be better or less well suited to our purposes, but that is all. To be sure, there was deep disagreement, even among the ancient Greeks, about this way of thinking about the relation of pastoralist and flock. In the same dialogue in which Plato has Socrates describe the good shepherd taking care of the sheep, one of his interlocutors, Thrasymachus,[10] responds that to describe the situation this way is to get the wrong end of the stick completely. The shepherd does not keep the sheep healthy for the *sheep's benefit*, but for his own profit. Who, one might ask, eventually eats whom in this relationship? This makes the situation not so different from that of my father and the locomotive. If he were feeling expansive my father might have said he took care of the locomotive 'for the sake of the smooth operation of the production process, and thus the general human benefits that accrued from that', or if he were feeling small-minded he might say he did it for his own sake, in order not to lose his job. He would not say he was looking out for the welfare of the locomotive or keeping it in operation for *its* benefit.

Another version of this situation can be seen to arise if one thinks about what I said above, about pastoralists learning to 'improve' the animals in their care, perhaps by selective breeding. 'Improve' seems in this context to mean make them better *for us*, better suited to the purposes we set for them. We bred them for more meat or milk, or thicker wool, and so that they would be more fertile and more tractable, because that was what *we* wanted them for.

Thrasymachus, however, seems to me to make a serious mistake when asking whether the shepherd cultivates the welfare of the sheep for its sake or for his own sake. This formulation suggests that it must be one or the other, but not both, that these are strict alternatives, when clearly the most interesting thing about animal husbandry is that, if practised correctly, it can be both. Even to make that distinction as a strict one is, to some extent, to miss the point, because humans and domesticated animals stand to each other in a symbiotic relation in which the good of one cannot strictly be distinguished (overall) from that of the other. The process of domestication, one might say, is a two-way street at the end of which both the domesticating human group and the domesticated animal become co-dependent. When Montaigne was entertained by his cat, he was right to wonder whether his cat was not, perhaps, being entertained by him.[11] Even if it is true that the humans eat the sheep, it might also be true that the humans could not continue to survive without the sheep, and this dependence may structure the humans' behaviour in deep ways. The answer to the question 'who eats whom' does not completely settle the issue because after all, parasites, as their name indicates, live by feeding off us, and yet we would be loath to think of all of human history, including the poems of Homer, the Cathedral at Chartres, and Beethoven's last string quartets, as just a means for the present generation of tapeworms, bedbugs, and *Entamoeba histolytica* to reproduce themselves through history by feasting on us.

So pastoralism does look something like what we call 'work' in that it is an exhausting activity that contributes in an objective way to subsistence. There are some differences, for instance, the ethos of care that seems to be a necessary part of this regime. It is also the case that pastoralists may well not receive any money for their activity, but there is one feature of their way of life which distinguishes it from that of hunters and foragers and which seems to constitute a precursor to monetary payment. For pastoralists something like a wage or salary is closer to being at any rate a permanent possibility. A herder of animals can be more or less wealthy, and this wealth can take a *countable* form, so that it is possible to compare the wealth of one with that of another. In a way, only when that becomes possible does the very idea of 'wealth' begin to make sense. The man who has five camels is richer than the one who has three; just count the camels. This means I can offer to watch over your fifty sheep for a month, *if you give me three of them at the end of that time.* I can then offer to watch over someone else's fifty sheep for two months, *provided he gives me* six sheep. By the end of the year, I could in principle hire – there would seem to be no other word for it – someone else to watch over *my* flock (as it now is), offering him some sheep as payment. Think of the compulsive mentioning of specific numbers of sheep and the obsession with increasing one's flock which can be found in the stories about the patriarchs in the Judeo-Christian Bible. None of this need be the way things work, but it becomes possible that they might begin to work in this way. Nothing similar is at all usual in societies devoted to hunting or foraging, for a number of reasons. First, there is the sheer diversity of the things people in such societies do to get food, the great variety of the food they consume, and the relatively egalitarian access to what food there is. How do you compare easily collected nuts, which are available in the environment for most of the year in most places and which anyone can pick up, with honey that is extremely difficult to find and to collect, or with a fish one can with moderate care take with a net, or with a gazelle which it takes two men in the prime of life to run down, or a kudu that is one of a herd of 100 which a large group of hunters have driven over a cliff at the conclusion of a long and difficult hunt and now must distribute or divide? There is no obvious common unit. The next step is taken when a group of pastoralists decides that, say, twenty sheep can be exchanged for one camel. We seem clearly on the way to money, which, one will recall, in Latin is *pecunia*, derived from the word for cattle (*pecus*).

Agriculture

The third mode of subsistence is agriculture, in the broad sense, including horticulture, the beginnings of which go back millennia. This mode of obtaining subsistence has dominated our way of life for a very long time: even into the nineteenth century by far the majority of the population in most Western countries was engaged in agricultural labour of one sort or another (although this will probably have included some raising of livestock). What is striking, looking at it from the outside, is how laborious farming is as a way to make a living. Working in a rice-paddy or a wheat field simply requires much more exertion, of a more sustained kind, than do most forms of hunting or pastoralism (where they are possible). The question why the human species adopted systematic agriculture in the first place is a very good one; as far as I know there is no consensus among experts on the answer to this question. Once agriculture, especially the virtual monoculture of one of the classic staple crops, is established, though, one can see why people growing up in the dense network of social dependence which characterises such societies had little choice in the matter but to continue. There have, of course, in most places been families of relatively independent farmers, although in many cases even for these one might ask what choice they had in a natural world which had been reconfigured in the interests of increased agricultural productivity. This would have the result of making subsistence by simple hunting and gathering as difficult as possible. Rice-paddies make poor hunting grounds for most prey.

Nevertheless, no matter what one might think of the situation of such 'free' agriculturalists, it remains true that historically a very significant amount of agricultural labour has always been more or less coerced, though how this coercion is configured differs in different societies. Historically, many societies used slaves, war-captives, and condemned criminals for agricultural work. Here the coercion is visible in the clearest and most immediate way: individuals are chained together in a field and whipped until they plant or harvest tobacco, sugar, or cotton, or they are chained to a millstone to grind cultivated grain, or put on a treadmill and whipped until they turn the wheel. Humans have, however, been ingenious in inventing ever more sophisticated and indirect forms of coercion, and in institutionalising what is sometimes coyly called 'dependent labour'. There are helots, indentured labourers, serfs, debt-bondsmen, coolies, indentured servants, dependent tenants, villeins, *coloni*, to name just a few. In many traditional societies large numbers of peasant cultivators are 'bound to the soil' (*glebae adscripti* to use the medieval Latin term) as serfs in feudal Europe were, meaning that they were legally forbidden from leaving their holding and were required to cultivate it and to give a fixed proportion of the harvest to the feudal master. They would, of course, also be subject to a huge mass of customary duties, including forced labour of various kinds (*corvée*). The actual variety of specific provisions that govern obligations of peasants to feudal lords is infinitely great, but it seems fair to say that 'necessity' here takes the form of a combination of the visible need to continue to feed one's family and the threat that the feudal lord will bring to bear the huge military and legal apparatus of direct coercion which he or she (or they, for instance a community of monks) have at their disposal.

It is certainly true that the serf in the Middle Ages worked hard, even very hard, but, of course, he or she did not have a job. Being someone's serf is not a job, not even a full-time job; it is a status, which is something completely different. A status is something I can acquire in various ways, for instance by being born the serf of some lord, and it is certainly something I cannot change *ad libitum*. When I say I 'have' a job, the natural assumption we, at any rate, are inclined to make is that there is a 'me' who also works at that job. I am a subject and have some power of free choice, but a serf isn't a 'me' who happens at the moment to be a serf; certainly he or she is not a subject who has somehow 'decided' to be a serf, but someone who is *essentially* a serf.

In a way one can see those with a 'vocation' as very much like serfs in that they have a close identification with their calling. The Dominican clerics were, following a false folk etymology, not just the bond-servants but the 'dogs of the Lord' (*domini canes*). The Jesuits expected members to obey Providence acting 'through their superiors' as if they were 'corpses' (*cadaver*) with no will of their own. This religious injunction to turn oneself into the servant/slave of one's deity conforms to a doctrine, held by some religious thinkers, that being the deity's slave was actually perfect freedom, and the only freedom available to humans.

Serfs are not tied to feudal lords by bonds of obligation that run in one direction only. At least in principle there are things that their lords owe them, too, although the gap between principle and reality here may be very wide, and serfs in any case have virtually no power to force their lords to give them inconvenient traditional benefits. These purported benefits – such as a new suit of clothing every other year or the opening of the lord's fields for gleaning the day after the harvest – and the serfs' gifts – a barrel of beer on the marriage of the lord's first son or daughter, or the first brace of partridges they catch in the autumn – are not considered to be payments or exchanges that are equivalent to payments, but simply existing custom-ary obligations that derive from the respective status of lord and serf. They are things that derive from, maintain, and reinforce the existing relation in general, rather than specific forms of *quid pro quo*. Status relations are not in general based on anything like what we would call a 'contract', and the interactions that maintain them are not regulated by individual acts of exchange of things taken to be economic-ally equivalent or 'of the same value'. Certainly the serf gets no pay. When feudal obligations of goods and services – in either direction – began to be converted into cash payments, as they eventually did, that in itself was a sign that the feudal world was already on its way out.

Craft Production

The traditional historical four-stage schema moves directly from agriculture to commerce (or industry), but there is another mode of work that is not completely captured in this schema, and that is individual craft production. The individual artisan – potter, carpenter, or dressmaker – is not engaged in agriculture, but she or he is also not part of a highly mechanised form of industrial production. Craft production is overlooked in many of the historical schemas because it is thought to be an inherently subsidiary sector in a society in which another form of production (usually agriculture or industry) dominates. The whole society could in principle live on hunting and foraging, on herding animals, on growing food, or on agro-industry, but not exclusively on the activity of individuals in small workshops crafting one-of-a-kind leather boots or musical instruments or pieces of furniture. Nevertheless, craft production is theoretically important if only because it remains the natural source of an idea which still has a strong purchase on many people, that is the idea of 'pride in one's work' or 'pride in good workmanship'. This notion still seems to inform our assumptions about the satisfactions which work *should* bring to the worker. It is not, of course, that hunters take no pride in their skill – although in some of the more egalitarian hunter–gatherer groups there is strong social pressure against expressing anything at all like that. It is also not the case that the agriculturalist is embarrassed or ashamed of working on the land, but that is not at all the same thing. A ferocious attachment to the particular little strip of land which the family cultivates is the characteristic attitude of farmers; it is rather artisans who are proud of their work.

During the past century or two, fashion has moved back and forth between an aesthetic based on industrial production and one derived from craft practice. For a very long time machine production seemed to have an inherent fascination for people. On the side of a building in Cambridge one can just barely see the outlines of an old advertisement, which, to judge by the lettering, must date from before World War II. It advertises a brand of bread, praising it on the grounds that it is 'entirely machine made'. Much bread still is, I assume, 'machine made', but no one, these days, would think of citing this as a special reason to buy it. We are much more likely to be attracted by 'artisanal bread', 'craft ales', 'small batch whiskeys', or anything 'hand-picked' (when used of any fruit or vegetable, for instance, grapes for wine-making), that is by products that purport to be made with the individual attention to detail and high regard for quality that is thought to be possible only in craft production. In a way one can see a certain amount of the social criticism of industrial work as deriving from a failure to find in it the virtues that were thought to exist in craft production: a high level of suitability for individual and potentially idiosyncratic purposes ('made to measure'), a high level of quality in general in the product, the ability of the producer to express herself in the work process and the product, and to take pride in the result. In the writings of several nineteenth- and early-twentieth-century thinkers one can see a certain vacillation about whether we should look 'backwards' and try to make industrial work more individually expressive as it purportedly is in craft production, or whether we should drive 'forwards' with increasing industrialisation of the work processes so that the workers are eventually able to stand back completely from the fully automated processes and be free to seek self-expression and self-affirmation elsewhere.

3   The Anthropology and Economics of Work

The previous two chapters have painted a rather grim picture of work and its place in human life, at any rate since the time when humans became sedentary and then eventually began systematically to practise agriculture in a way that made us dependent on it. It seems that the necessity for a society to produce enough for subsistence trickled down through an almost unsurveyably varied series of complex paths to a highly local form of coercion which forces me in *this* specific situation to exert myself strenuously at an unpleasant task that I would prefer not to do. Is the situation really as dismal as this might be taken to suggest?

Since this is a general question, presumably it needs an answer in terms of something like a philosophical anthropology, that is, an account of what kind of creature or living thing a human being is and the properties which such a creature usually, or invariably, exhibits.

Lazybones

A lot of popular economic thought – meaning by that the kind of thing ordinary people unreflectively say about employment – and the pronouncements made by some political figures seem to depend on the assumption that people are naturally work-shy. Human beings, some think, are inherently lazy; strenuous exertion is something they self-evidently avoid. The supporters of this view might claim that simple observation is enough to confirm this. Offer the workers at a factory the chance of working 40 hours a week, or 45 hours for the same wages, and see which they will invariably prefer. Historically, too, the general course of human inventiveness has been in the direction of finding ways to do the things we wish to do while saving human exertion: we domesticated animals to carry our burdens for us, then eventually replaced them with machines. No laboratory or institute is now doing research to discover *more* exhausting ways for us to tie our own shoes or cook our meals. This is true despite the fact that large numbers of people are also joining health clubs to get the exercise that a human animal needs to remain fit. Finally, if one considers the history of the utopian dreams which humans have had and expressed through history, one constant repeated motif is that of the relief from work. In the western European peasant imagination this is illustrated by such fantasies as 'the Land of Cockaigne', depicted in the famous sixteenth-century painting by Bruegel the Elder (now in the Alte Pinakothek, Munich). In this painting a group of peasants are lying around on the ground, feasting on food that does not need to be grown or prepared. Eggs have small legs, and run toward the somnolent human figures; their shells are already broken open and they are helpfully provided with protruding knives to make them easier to eat. All the peasants in the picture have to do is open their mouths and fowl, already roasted, fly into them of their own accord. Following on from this, one might think that McDonald's, Burger King, and Kentucky Fried Chicken are, from the viewpoint of the customers (although not of the staff), the realisation of a dream. Some may think these institutions to be a kind of diabolical transformation of this old peasant fantasy into a living hell, but they obviously are attractive to a great many people. The fantasy is of a world without effort (and thus certainly without the strenuous effort of systematically organised work).

The implications of this line of thought are clearly that if work really is necessary for human survival and people want to survive in the long run, then there needs to be something that acts to resist and thwart their natural tendency to live in the moment and give way to their inherent tendencies toward complete indolence. There would seem to be three possible paths here: make people work by (direct or indirect) coercion, persuade them to work by appeals to reason, and finally incite them to work through the provision of (positive or negative, non-rational) incentives.

Coercion

To begin with, it is important to note that direct coercion in the true sense of the term is counterproductive, or at any rate highly inefficient, in the sphere of work. There is such a thing as real physical coercion: I can force you to push a button by taking your hand and exerting such pressure on it that the hand presses the button down. Similarly I can stand over a slave with a spade and, if I am sufficiently strong, physically bend his arm to the ground and try to force the spade in his hand into the soil, but after doing this a few times, I might decide that it is easier to use the spade myself. This is not to deny the existence of coercion in social relations, but merely to point out that what we call 'coercion' in work contexts generally does not take this direct form. When we speak of forcing someone to work we mean that we actively create a situation in which the person in question has no reasonable alternative but to do the work in question. If I stand over a slave, and whip her until she works, what I do is leave her no reasonable alternative but to labour, though, of course, what she will consider 'reasonable' might not be what I think is reasonable. Whipping can be assumed to be more efficient to the extent to which I do not have to whip her *all the time* (and to the extent to which raising a whip is easier than doing whatever the assigned task is). It would be even more efficient for the slave-holders if they needed merely to issue verbal threats rather than actual physical beatings. Obviously killing a slave is not a way of forcing her to work, although (credibly) threatening to kill her may give her an incentive to work and being seen to kill her may give other slaves a similar incentive.

In addition to encountering resistance, direct coercion or the threat of it can backfire, because cruelty can actually generate active opposition at least in those capable of it. Not everyone is able to resist all the time, but some might be some of the time. This is a further reason to try to avoid direct coercion, at any rate unless one can be absolutely sure that those who might be incited to counter-aggression are permanently disabled from acting on this motive – without being impaired in their labour-power, and how exactly is one to do that?

Many slave-holders were sadists, and the very institution clearly had a brutalising effect on all who participated in it, but from the sheer point of view of *work*, the slave-holder does not naturally wish to exterminate or physically harm the slaves, but rather wants to control their labour-power, which means that the slaves have to have some. This, in a sense, is one of the paradoxes of slavery, that for it to be profitable, the slave-holder must want his slaves to be vital and active (for instance in working a plantation), but never independent. It would make good sense to enlist the workers themselves in making the work regime run efficiently, if I could, because the more I can do that the less I need to use my whip. Well, good luck with that project in a regime of slave labour. The more one thinks about it, the more difficult it seems to run an efficient slave regime. All regimes that are not more or less pure forms of slave labour have to have or make room for something else.

We know that humans in fact react differently to 'natural' obstacles and to those which they can see have been created by other people, and particularly they discriminate between natural obstacles and those created by other people specifically in order to thwart their desires or force them to act in a certain way. They especially dislike this last kind of hindrance. Thus, individuals and groups who are producing skewed incentive structures will, if they are clever, try to hide behind the fiction that these are just 'facts of nature' rather than imposed human constructs. Human ingenuity has a field-day here. Foucault in his book *Discipline and Punish*[1] discusses various ways in which the structuration of space itself can become a form of indirect control. Part of the interest in this is that if one can assign some of the coercive function to anonymous features of the situation rather than the direct action of some individual, the possible rage of those being coerced can be displaced, diffused, diverted, or nullified. One of Foucault's own major examples of this is the panopticon. This is a form of building which maximises the visibility of the people who are to be kept under surveillance there, such as a prison. In a panopticon the structure of the space makes the interior of every cell clearly visible to anyone who happens to be in a central observation tower, and also makes it clear to each inmate that this is the case. Conversely, precautions are taken to ensure that the inmates do not know who at any point is in the observation post, or indeed if anyone is in there at all. In this case it is the building itself that is a means of coercion, because the inmates never know when they are in fact being observed and must assume they are under surveillance all the time. Note, too, that the effect will be almost the same, even if the central observation tower is unmanned (provided that the inmates cannot see that). It is not, then, the individual guard who is thwarting the inmate's wishes in a direct way.

This example is taken from Foucault's account of the prison system, but it is easy to see how an analogous account could be given of work-places and for that matter of other central features of many systems for organising work.

Reasoning

Let us now put aside for the moment regimes of work that visibly depend to an overwhelming extent on coercion or the threat of the direct infliction of pain, and consider the second of the three paths to counteracting laziness, the appeal to reason. One might hope that reason in the form of foresight, more specifically of calculations about the future, might be mobilisable to this end. However, is there really anything inherently more rational about preferring the future to the present? Some of us may be inveterately like the cicada in La Fontaine's fable, and happy to sing all day during the summer without preparing for the winter, rather than like the ant who hoards against the future. It is possible that enough of us will be susceptible to the force of the observation that we must plant the seeds now, if we are not to starve in the coming winter, for the group as a whole not to perish. Perhaps consideration of the future does in fact outweigh present enjoyment for many, but does this show that the priority given to the future is rational?

There are at least three difficulties with appeals to reason. The first is that what counts as reason in any real practical context is much less well-defined than many philosophers seem to believe. After all, 'we must plant the seeds now' may seem obvious enough, but if it is announced, for instance, by the head of the village, it effectively means '*you all* must *now* go to plant the seeds in *those* fields', which is another kettle of fish entirely. This remains the case even if what the village elder says is in fact perfectly true. The more complex the economy, the more untransparent and debatable the connections involved. Second, appeals to reason have little chance of success if the society in which they are made is itself visibly a crude insult to the very idea of reasonableness. Thus, Hegel[2] explains the reason why the

attempt by medieval thinkers to appeal to reason in discussing any social arrangements seems to us moderns to be
merely ludicrous. Medieval society can't be represented as
rational because it wasn't and did not even pretend to be: it
was a mass of singularities based on accidents of geography
and biology, historical anomalies, relations of force, and
religious fantasies of various kinds. This is why, for many
of us, reading medieval philosophers like Thomas Aquinas is
much like the experience of hearing *'Dieu le veult'* shouted
loudly in unison by massed crusading knights waving their
swords. There is, of course, nothing inherently wrong with
shouting loudly in unison – it might raise spirits and intimi-
date enemies – but one should not confuse it with reasoning.
Since reason clearly wasn't going to work, one needed tradition, faith, fear, and so on. Hegel thinks that medieval
society does have a kind of rationality, because it was a
necessary part of a process that eventually led to the modern
world, but this is something that can be discovered only
retrospectively from a point of view which no one who lived
in the Middle Ages could possibly have occupied. So, for
him, one of the main advances of the French Revolution was
not that it created a rational society – it clearly did not – but
that it for the first time formulated sharply and explicitly the
idea (and enunciated the political demand) that all of society
be treated as if it were fully rational. Whether or not Hegel
was right about that – didn't Plato imagine that a society
could be thoroughly rational? – and whether or not one
accepts the details of this account, it seems beyond doubt
that if you know you are getting much more than your
reasonable share of the social pie, you have good grounds

to think twice before appealing to reason in economic and political contexts.

Finally, everyone knows the unreliability and sheer weakness of reason – even if everyone agrees on what it 'demands' – as a motivation to do anything, especially to do anything which goes against our own deep-seated impulses and preferences. As noted, too, the more abstract and complex the reasoning becomes, the more diverse factors it tries to take into account and the further into the future it attempts to peer, the weaker its already feeble motivational power becomes. So if our human inclination to non-activity is as strong as the proponents of this line of thought suggest, then the actual ability of considerations of 'reason' to move people to work, except in truly exceptional circumstances of immediate and visible urgency, will be very low indeed.

Incentives

What, then, about incentivisation? To some extent one can see the appeal to reason as a kind of incentive: what, in a sense, could be a *stronger* incentive to ploughing this spring than the perfectly reasonable prediction that if we don't, we will all starve in the winter? Since that kind of case has already been considered, though, let's put it aside and look at other possible, non-rational incentives that could be offered for work. I note that attention to incentives in a way moves us on considerably in the direction of a more realistic discussion, partly because it brings into focus the social and political dimension of the question about the necessity of work. One can in principle construe reason as some kind of abstract, disembodied, and inherently impartial feature of the world, and thus try to see the appeal to reason as in some sense standing outside the specific social constellation of power. I think it is wrong to construe reason and the appeals to reason in this way, but I don't think it is daft or incoherent. However, no one thinks that incentives grow on trees or that they hover about until discovered in a celestial realm. In most concrete cases, certainly in paradigm cases, we speak of an incentive when someone is offering something to someone else, to another person or group, conditional upon their doing or not doing something. It is the group of people who are opening a new factory in an unattractive location who must offer something (a positive incentive) to potential workers to encourage them to come to work in that factory. In our fully monetarised society that will probably be something like a sum of money as a recruitment bonus or the offer of a higher wage than expected, but it need not be anything like that. Thus I could offer to delouse anyone who would scratch the part of my back which I cannot easily reach, or I could offer to pray for their soul, or point out to them that everyone will come to have a better opinion of them if they show themselves eager to be of service. Or I can offer a negative incentive, starting with a weak one, such as that if they fail to do what I want I will have a worse opinion of them than I do, and then stronger and stronger incentives, which, if they become severe enough, can eventually shade over into direct coercion, such as threatening physical abuse to those who wish to leave my employment, or who try to organise a labour union in my factory.

As we have noted, the basic model for speaking about incentives is one in which one person or group (a master or employer) is giving an incentive to another person or group. What, however, if people could be brought to give *themselves* an incentive to work, that is, if they could be brought in some way to internalise the idea that working was good in itself or that they were good people precisely by virtue of working hard? What if they could come to adopt what is sometimes called a work-ethic, that is, the idea that work was not just necessary, but in some sense good in itself, or at least something that one ought to find good in itself? As people nowadays might put it, what if one could cause people to adopt 'diligent labourer' as part of their core identity or sense of self, so that they came to approve of themselves only if they worked hard for its own sake and felt guilty if they were not working hard, even when it was not strictly necessary? This view of work was not at all widely held in the ancient Greco-Roman world. Work was for slaves, and the characteristic of a free man (the theorisation of human life explicitly focused on the life of the adult *male* citizen) was the ability to lead – or at least to take some part in – a life of leisure. Poverty may not have been considered to be per se shameful, but was thought to constitute a limitation to one's ability to lead a fully honourable and good human life.[3] Some particularly strenuous lives were admired, like that of Heracles, but they were admired because they were victorious in highly dramatic set-piece confrontations with other humans (usually inveterate evil-doers) or with individual animate monsters, and because by ridding the earth of these nuisances they contributed to the common good. But going out on a specific expedition to kill the Hydra, and then spending long periods of time in sloth and gluttony, like Heracles – who was known both for his heroic deeds and for his extreme *gourmandise* – is not actually very much like engaging in the hard, unglamorous day-to-day grind of, say, agricultural work. As far as I know, there are no representations in ancient literature of figures who are presented as admirable *because* they raise themselves up from poverty by their own hard work, much less any glorification of the process of working hard itself, regardless of its outcome.

Solidarity

One very important kind of incentive to work is solidarity, so perhaps that could eventually give rise to some form of work-ethic. The term 'solidarity' originally referred to legal obligations, not to any subjective state of human feelings. In Roman law the 'solidarity' of a family meant that all members of the same family were co-responsible for debts incurred by other members of the same family. Because all the members of a particular group are in fact held responsible, they begin to feel themselves to be responsible for all parts of some collective endeavour, and hence come to see themselves as having a shared interest in certain outcomes. Durkheim in the nineteenth century took this general concept and applied it in particular to the forms of collective responsibility and shared interests that develop in connection with particular ways in which people work together.[4] People who work together, especially small groups who work together for relatively long periods, tend to develop the expectation that members of the group will not let the others down, that they will pull together and do their part.

One finds ideas like this remarkably early in Western literature, in fact in one of the very first works that have been preserved: Homer's *Iliad* (Book XV). While the Greeks are besieging the city of Troy, the Greek hero Achilles, the best warrior on either side, decides he has been insulted by the leader of the expedition, Agamemnon, and withdraws from the fighting. The Trojans are then able to beat the Greeks back, away from the walls of the city to their beached ships. Aias (Ajax), another Greek military leader, who is not the swiftest bunny in the hutch but is an especially stalwart and dependable warrior, appeals to their sense of shame (*aidos*), calling for them to stand by each other:

> Friends, be men and set up shame (*aido*) in your hearts,
> be ashamed (*aideisthe*) to abandon one another in the
> fierce battle,
> for if men maintain that sense of shame (*aidomenon*)
> more of them stay safe than are killed. [*Iliad* XV, 561–563]

The appeal to stand by each other and the accumulated use of words derived from 'shame' (three times in three lines) in this passage is very striking.

A similar ethos can arise in work contexts, especially among groups who know each other well in other contexts and also work closely together over long periods on collective projects; they quickly learn that they have to depend on each other in a large number of informal ways. In such a group, feelings that 'We are all in this together, and must therefore help each other out' arise in ways that seem to be perfectly spontaneous. No worker wants to be seen to be a slacker, and thus each has a strong incentive to be seen not to be letting the others down. It is not unimportant that this is connected to visibility. Aias was right to speak of 'shame', which is a fear of being *seen* to be something (a deserter, slacker, skiver). This does not mean that this sense cannot eventually be internalised into a form of guilt,[5] but it retained, even into the late twentieth century, traces of this origin. There is, of course, a huge difference between what the workers would take to be a form of slacking off and what the management and owners would characterise in that way, and for workers only one's co-workers' opinion mattered.

Work-relations, of course, do not always generate feelings of solidarity. Another very early Greek poet, Hesiod (late eighth to early seventh century BC), begins one of his poems by distinguishing two kinds of strife (*eris*), a good kind and a bad. The bad one expresses itself in wars, brawls, and legal disputes. The good strife, however,

> ... incites even a useless man to work
> for if he who is not working sees another who is rich,
> ploughing and planting diligently
> and setting his house in order, then one neighbour will vie
> with the neighbour who is pursuing wealth
> and this strife is good for mortals
> and potter is angry with potter and builder with builder
> and one beggar is envious of another and one bard of
> another.[6]

If the basic state of people who are on the same team, in the same army or working together as a group is solidarity, individual beggars are more likely to compete with each other. A high level of individual competition, often organised into public *agones* (contests), was a well-recognised feature of life in the ancient world, and there was a clear further recognition of the envy that was a natural concomitant of this social formation. In a way one can see a lot of ancient philosophy as trying to create impersonal ideals that can be the objects of human aspiration, thus replacing potentially toxic forms of individual competition. Rather than competing directly against each other, men (because it was mostly men) are to be encouraged to aspire to the greatest possible state of ... wisdom, virtue, knowledge, imperturbability, an aspiration that can be collectively and collaboratively pursued.

The solidarity of co-workers is a problematic phenomenon for owners and management. On the one hand, many work processes would virtually come to a halt unless the immediate workers displayed some minimal willingness to help one another out, even in ways not strictly required by law and contract and not strictly enforceable. There seems no doubt but that the greater the solidarity among workers in the work-place, the greater the efficiency. So, presumably, managers should welcome anything that increases workers' sense of being involved in a common cause in which each must be able to depend on the others. Unfortunately – for the owners – solidarity cannot reliably be expected to remain within foreseeable and clearly delimited bounds, but can often spill over into other areas, and one of the great fears of managers must be that the mutual aid which is natural and essential in the work-place could become the basis of possible resistance to various measures which the managers might wish to introduce, but which the workers see to be directly contrary to their own interests. The ultimate nightmare is that mutual aid might perhaps lead to a wider, eventually political, mobilisation of the workers.

The generation of envy, as described by Hesiod, is still a formidable tool in the hands of managers, precisely because it tends to break down solidarity. During a strike at the Fairless Works where my father was employed, after a long period of tortuous negotiations the management suddenly pulled out of its hat a special and fantastically generous offer of a wage increase for the painters, a small group who were generally looked down on by the rest of the workers because their work was thought to be easy and very well paid given how unskilled it was. I can still hear the incredulous and slightly angry shouts of some of the mechanics: 'The *painters*?!' The idea was presumably to divert the workers' attention from the general confrontation with management, to split them and to cause them to begin enviously attacking one another.[7] In this particular case, the representatives of the union saw through the stratagem and calmed everyone down, but one could clearly see why the company preferred not to engage in blanket negotiations covering the whole industry, but rather wished to conduct them piecemeal, plant by plant and union by union, and also why they liked to subdivide the workers into as many different categories as possible so they could play one off against the other.

Because visibility is such a salient feature in generating and maintaining solidarity, it is not surprising that it seems to be generated most intensely and most persistently among relatively small groups of co-workers, where the contribution of each is in fact immediately visible to all others. If your work-group is composed of ten people and your job is to move steel girders which require two people to lift, everyone quickly learns who is stronger, who is quicker, and, most important of all, who is cooperative and is making an effort and who is trying to slack off. At some point spontaneous solidarity can be transmuted into what is called 'peer pressure'. However, the bigger and more unsurveyable the group, and, in particular, the more unstable the membership, the less visibility there is, and the greater the possibility of slacking off (also called, variously, 'skylarking', 'idling', 'skiving', 'coasting', 'loafing about') without being seen.[8]

The Work-Ethic

How does the aboriginal shame-based solidarity turn into the work-ethic? Nietzsche thought, roughly, that the answer was masochism. Particularly weak people forced to live in close proximity with crowds of others had no outlet for their natural and perfectly comprehensible aggression, because if they had expressed it, they would have received from the strong people much worse than they were able to dish out, so they had to learn to turn it against themselves, and eventually to internalise it. They developed what he called 'ascetic ideals' – that is, positive valorisations of this ability to turn one's aggression into something internal directed against oneself. To learn to engage in strenuous work for its own sake is precisely to adopt such an ideal.[9] Such glorification of work is a way for people to let out their aggressions against someone who, in contrast to the other people around them, can be counted on *not* to retaliate against them in kind and in double or treble measure, namely against themselves.

The sociologist Max Weber, who was a keen student of the writings of Nietzsche, gave an analysis of the origin of the work-ethic which is not incompatible with Nietzsche's, but slightly more fine-grained and differently focused. For Nietzsche, Christianity itself, with its cult of humility and non-retaliation, is a highly developed form of the 'ascetic ideal'. Weber, however, focuses more specifically on sixteenth- and seventeenth-century developments in Christianity. The Book of Genesis makes it clear that work is a necessity imposed by God on humanity (as a result of Adam's sin in Eden). This in itself, however, is not sufficient to give anyone a special incentive to work with particular assiduousness. In fact, on the older Catholic view this passage means that work is merely a grim servile necessity and a punishment for sin. As a divine punishment one might have to accept it, perhaps even with good grace, but that does not mean that one attributes any positive value to it. Even if people think that it behoves a justly condemned criminal to accept punishment willingly, this does not mean that anyone thinks the punishment is *in itself* good, or that one should actively pursue and cultivate it for its own sake. Work, then, has a (religiously based) 'meaning' – it is a punishment – but don't look for anything else in it. The ideal would be to reduce it as much as possible. One has to work if one wishes to eat – that was clear – but only an imbecile would seek out work for its own sake, or would define their identity through a job or career. In fact, on a very widely shared medieval Catholic view, the life that was best and most full of meaning was a life not of work, but of religious contemplation, such as purportedly provided by certain monastic communities. Even today Orthodox Jews consider a life devoted completely to study of the Law to be superior to any form of work. Work, for Catholics, might play some part even in the religious life, because it was imposed by God as a punishment, and even the religious must therefore come to terms with it, but the details of this work were insignificant in themselves and work itself was to be completely subordinated to prayer, contemplation, and the performance of complex rites. Some might be called to a religious life, but that was a special vocation to something higher and was different from the general fact that (in principle, even if not in practice) after the Fall everyone was forced to work.

In contrast to this, Max Weber suggested that early Protestantism, and in particular Calvinism, represented an important shift in the conception of and attitudes toward work. As a result of a complex historical development (part of which was a series of understandable human distortions of Calvin's original theology), 'work' for the Calvinist came to be the domain in which one proves to oneself one's own worth; one should focus as much as possible on working as hard as one can, and being as frugal and parsimonious as possible in other parts of one's life. For Calvin, people could be called to particular jobs in the world; these jobs were then construed as having religious meaning in themselves and in the details of their performance. Instead of reserving true religiosity for a more or less separate and distinct sphere, or associating it with particular ritual acts, this diffuses ultimate meaning and sentiments of absolute seriousness throughout the world of work. Calvinists practise a special diligence in the details of work and a denigration of idleness and spontaneous enjoyment; Weber calls this 'innerworldly asceticism'.

Paradoxically, the part of Calvin's theory that had the greatest effect on the genesis of the work-ethic was his doctrine of predestination, which held that God had 'predestined' each person before their birth to salvation or eternal damnation. This judgement was irrevocable and thus we, during the time when we were living our lives, could do nothing to change it. It was also hidden from us. No one could know who was saved and who was not. The one thing one could see, however, was that certain people, against all the odds, turned out to be highly successful, while others, seemingly equally gifted and in equally good circumstances, failed. Such signal success was a sign of God's grace and favour. One might think that the consequences of this would be quietistic: since some people are predestined by God to success and others to failure, in this life and in the next, why work? But in fact, Weber claims, the real motivational effect was the reverse: every Calvinist was under the most enormous internal psychological pressure to demonstrate that he or she was in fact predestined to be saved, by being a spectacularly vivid external success in the world. Whatever work one did, one needed to treat it not merely as if it was a burdensome necessity (as Catholics purportedly did), but as something to which one was *called*. To be called to *this* work meant not just to discharge it correctly or even excellently but to identify oneself with it. There should be a kind of professional whole-heartedness in everything a Calvinist does. That is the sympathetic way of putting it. A rather less sympathetic approach would point out that since for Calvin we are all, whether saved or damned, sinners who *deserve* damnation, and the saved are saved *despite* their sins, this is an invitation to unscrupulous ruthlessness. After all, nothing one could do could actually change God's predestined verdict, so the only sign of his election that is possible in this life was one's own unmerited, but spectacular, success. This amounted, psychologically speaking, to acting as if the salvation of one's soul depended not on acting in an especially moral way, but on the visibly successful outcome of whatever action one undertook. If one believed in God's providence and in the deep obscurity of his final purposes and 'ways' ('*deus absconditus*', another strongly held Calvinist doctrine), then precisely the visible manifestation of God's unmotivated judgement in the success of the scapegrace could become an edifying spectacle.

Weber does not claim that Calvinism 'causes' capitalism or even that it 'causes' the work-ethic. He is, in fact, very explicit in denying any such intention. Rather what he claims is that there is an 'elective affinity' between Calvinism and early entrepreneurial activity. This means that there will be a kind of reciprocal attraction between the two of them, if they find themselves in the same social environment: an entrepreneur will find, as we might say, Calvinism more congenial than, say, Catholicism, if these are the two major religious options available, and Calvinists will see in the domain of economic enterprise a sphere of activity that they can easily make sense of in their own religious terms.

Weber's account is very much focused on entrepreneurs, and it is not completely clear how and why the work-ethic should be expected to have the same attraction for factory-workers. Then, too, although Weber is clear that he is not giving a causal account, still one might wonder whether the monumental scepticism about or complete indifference to highly specific theological beliefs like those of Calvinism, and the virtual collapse of their social presence, which are characteristic of most Western societies in the twenty-first century, would affect the work-ethic, and, if so, how exactly. The loss of the religious significance which the work-ethic had for earlier generations is, however, for Weber one of the main ideological difficulties of the modern period. The world of work that the Puritans, who were one specific Calvinist sect, created to satisfy their demands for religious meaning had, he thought, by the start of the twentieth century acquired a kind of structural autonomy which made it to some extent independent of that original motivation and able to continue to exert a kind of compulsion on us. As Weber puts it, in a still basically Catholic society, the Puritan stood out as someone who *wanted*, for religious reasons, to be a person whose whole life was fundamentally oriented around intense work (*Berufsmensch*), but in our modern society we are *forced*, by the economic system the Puritans helped to create, to be people obsessively devoted to our careers, whether we want to be or not.[10] The economic system has stopped being the expression of a religious sentiment and become a form of meaningless coercion. Weber says that we have created a carapace for our lives which is hard as steel (*stahlhartes Gehäuse*, usually translated as 'iron cage'); it is constrictive and irritating and (now) meaningless, but we cannot remove it.

While we cannot now simply decide by *fiat* to rid ourselves of the work-ethic or to abstract ourselves from the economic system in which it is embedded, the system could collapse as a result of adventitious factors or from the weight of its own internal contradictions; the latter is, of course, the possibility explored more extensively by Marx, who thought that our system of ownership would eventually stifle increases in productivity to such an extent that it would have to be changed. A number of later thinkers have worried about another contradiction, one which has gradually developed between the work-ethic and some of the other demands of a contemporary capitalist economy. In his book *The Cultural Contradictions of Capitalism* (1976), Daniel Bell argued that capitalism had increasingly to become consumerist in order to maintain itself: it had to stimulate ever-increasing demand for a wider and wider variety of ever more exotic goods and services. This meant that it had actively to foster a kind of hedonism. Bell feared that the growing taste for luxury would eventually undermine the work-ethic and thus the psychological underpinnings of the whole system. How could the worker be an ascetic on the job and a luxury-crazed hedonist in her role as consumer? In retrospect, his fear seems to have been exaggerated and misplaced: 'Work hard, play hard' turns out to be psychologically less self-evidently intolerable than

Bell thought. In fact, innerworldly asceticism could relatively easily be replaced by a battery of other psychological
attitudes that were compatible with the maintenance and
further development of the existing system of work. Some
of these replacements might look like reactivations of more
archaic forms of reaction, such as an *agon*-like desire to be
seen to triumph over competitors, but some of them have a
distinctly more modern, even countercultural origin. In
their *The New Spirit of Capitalism*[11] (1999), Luc Boltanski
and Ève Chiapello show how management literature
since the 1980s has attempted, more or less successfully,
to co-opt much of the culturally inspired criticism of capitalist enterprise and to incorporate many of the central
concepts which critics once used to attack capitalism into a
discourse that glorifies the existing mode of production.
The watchwords used by large enterprises are no longer
discipline, sobriety, frugality, and prudence, but creativity,
individuality, initiative, and self-expression. What is
more, Boltanski and Chiapello argue that, like most good
ideologies, this one could even claim to have some appearance of being a description of reality, because new forms
of technology do permit some flexibility in working
conditions of a kind which had not been usual in earlier
periods. To be sure, the same electronic media which
permit personnel to work at home also make possible a
tighter electronic surveillance of them than has ever before
been possible, and the flexibility in working conditions is
gained at the cost of making jobs extremely precarious, but
the latter effect could be claimed to be simply the reverse
side of a new 'freedom'.

The Active Animal

Up to now, we have gone along, for the purposes of argument, with the assumption that humans are generally disinclined to exert themselves. But what if that is not the case? What if people are not inherently averse to exertion or even to work? It certainly does not seem far-fetched to think that humans are basically living creatures, and as living creatures, specifically as animals, they are just as 'naturally' active as they are at rest. As Dewey pointed out in his book *Art as Experience* (1932), the life of an animal is characterised by a rhythm of periods of activity interspersed with periods of rest, and too much of one is as bad, and as keenly resisted, as too much of the other. It is said that prisoners fear nothing more than solitary confinement, partly because of the lack of human companionship, but partly because of the associated enforced lack of activity. The natural rhythm of human life, one might think, has two parts, like the systole and diastole of the circulatory system. In the first part, having discovered obstacles or barriers to desired action, one confronts them and overcomes them with an eye to some further end which gives the whole process sense, and in the second part one enjoys the consequences of having overcome the obstacles and attained the projected end; it is a period in which one relaxes, restores oneself, is indolent, and begins tentatively to think of other things. It is an important part of this rhythm not that the obstacles disappear (say, magically), but that *I* overcome them by my own efforts, and what is more that I *see* that I have overcome them by my own efforts. If any part of this process is interrupted, blocked, or excessively extended, if the obstacles exceed my power to overcome them despite my exertions, perhaps I shall be irritated, but that is not because of a general disinclination to act, even to act in a strenuous way, but for some much more specific reason, such as that my rhythm of life has been disturbed.

Rhythm, Expression, and Drudgery

Human life is not just punctuated by teleological focused activity and relaxation – it has an expressive component built into its two-stage rhythm. In his *Lectures on Aesthetics*, Hegel gives a striking illustration of this when he describes a young boy throwing stones into a pool and watching as a circular pattern of ripples is created.[12] The ripples are perfectly symmetrical and thus have a certain kind of beauty, and the boy can rightly enjoy that beauty without thinking of anything else, but the real point, Hegel claims, is not that this beauty exists and that the boy sees it, but rather that he sees that *he* has created it by his own efforts, by throwing the stone into the water. He appreciates the fact that *he* has made his mark, through action, on the world. Hegel even claims that this desire to see oneself as having expressively affected the environment is not just a natural human tendency but a vital (he says 'absolute') human need.

The problem for humans is not how to get us up out of our inveterate state of lazing about and motivate us to do anything whatever. The a priori state of humanity is not swinish slumber, terminal lethargy, or Oblomovean indolence – Oblomov is an interesting character partly because his abnormal sloth makes him an *unusual* deviant.[13] Rather our natural state is being 'in process', at one stage or another, of the cycle of structured action and rest. This does not mean that there is no problem at all with the organisation of work in human societies, just that this problem takes a different form from that of asking how on earth one gets people to work at all. It is a specific problem about getting people to engage in *this* form of activity rather than in some other. If it really is the case that we have a natural tendency to action and to self-expression (as part of a larger pattern of action and rest), then how can we harness that as much as possible to the production of necessities of life, or at any rate not thwart it too much? And who is the appropriate 'we' in that statement?

It is perhaps true that humans dislike enforced excessive work, just as they dislike the enforced excessive leisure of solitary confinement in prison. They avoid drudgery, that is work that is uninterrupted, repetitive, and pointless. They also dislike being exploited and taken advantage of, that is working hard primarily for the benefit of someone to whom they are not bound by intimate bonds of love, friendship, or affinity. However, all of these are separate issues and it would be a mistake to infer from any of these attitudes that humans in general are innately indolent. If some kind of activity, even strenuous activity and the overcoming of obstacles, is part of a normal and healthy human life, there is no reason in principle to assume that work, the focused strenuous attempt to produce objective necessities, must always be something people will go to great lengths to avoid.

Division of Labour

To be sure, one might think that a certain problem arises from our desire for varied activity and the avoidance of repetitive drudgery. This might seem to be incompatible with one of the basic principles of modern economies, which is the division of labour. At one time, one individual artisan would have fashioned shoes by hand – individual pair by individual pair – performing all the necessary operations such as cutting the leather, stitching, attaching the heel, and boring the eyelets for the laces. Division of labour in a large factory subdivides these tasks so that one person does the cutting for all the shoes, another does the stitching, and so on. This is sometimes called the 'technical division of labour'. By instituting such a division of labour, it turns out, production can be increased (even presumably without any additional mechanisation). There is also a second form of division of labour, called the 'social' division of labour, which takes place not within a single productive process but between them. In a very small village, every family might bake its own bread in an individual or communal oven, and also make its own wooden clogs. In a somewhat larger village, one family might specialise in baking bread and another in making clogs, and there would then be some kind of exchange of these items between them. Obviously the two kinds of division can be combined.

Division of labour, however, is not in itself really incompatible with the human need for variety of activity, because it requires only a separation of *functions*. Initially, at least, this says nothing about the distribution of people among the various functions, about who will discharge the activity at each step, and there need not be any assumption that one specified person or group will be 'bound' to one task and only that one task all the time. We can make a clear distinction between division of *labour*, and distribution of *personnel* among divided jobs. We could easily imagine rotas in which workers were encouraged to move from one job to another, not perhaps day by day but month by month. Still, we might think that this is a superficial and unconvincing argument. After all, part of the reason usually given for division of labour is that it is a form of specialisation and that people who specialise in this way become especially expert and efficient by virtue of always doing the same thing. Some jobs require long training, and, almost equally importantly, workers get better at some jobs the longer they work at them.

Routine and Incremental Action

Let me introduce a very crude distinction between activities that are (mere) routine and, to use a relatively value-neutral term, activities that are 'incremental' (or, to use a slightly less value-neutral term, 'progressive').

The models for an 'incremental' activity are what takes place in the best of cases in such activities as learning to play the piano, to make a medical diagnosis, or to speak French. We have a clear (if idealised) conception of how the process of learning to play the piano is supposed to proceed. As we practise, we improve, and eventually we extend the range of different things we can do – we can play more complicated pieces in an ever wider variety of different idioms. Further, again in the ideal case, it would be natural to assume that as our performance improves, the pleasure we take in the activity also increases, as does our ability to appreciate good playing.

Not all actions in all contexts are at all like this idealised model of incremental action. If I work on an assembly line tightening bolts, I may get slightly better at doing this job the third day than I was the first, but after that no further improvement in the exercise of my task will be likely to be possible. The action of working becomes merely repetitive; it is routine. Such deeply routine action can be seen also to arise when the natural internal dynamic of incremental action is blocked, interrupted, suspended, or otherwise interfered with. If, for instance, I were to be forced to continue to practise the same bar in a piece of music again and again without ever being able to pass on to anything else, I might experience a similar blockage.

On the other hand, even boredom can become interesting in some contexts. I may wonder: how exactly does this fellow succeed in exercising that powerful narco-leptic effect he has, making me feel an almost irresistible urge to close my eyes and nod off when he begins to speak? Even drudgery can become interesting in small doses. That is, even routine, repetitive jobs can in some contexts become incremental if they are performed in sufficiently limited quantities, if enough movement of people between them is permitted, if they are sufficiently well remunerated, and if it is possible to see them as embedded in some not-so-routine projects. The problem with routine jobs is not anything inherent in them, but something about the *economic* system – the specific way in which profit is socially extracted – which underpays those who work at such jobs, oppresses them while they are working, and forces them to stay in these forms of employment permanently. The tip-off is the use of the term 'dead-end job'. This is not a term that describes some natural position in the labour-process, but very much something that is an artefact of our system of entitlements which gives a few individuals and corporations the power to extract profit and control the conditions of work. This system of entitlements is embedded in a wider structure of classes in our society which keeps routine jobs underpaid and restricts mobility. So one could in principle maintain variety of employment and division of labour, roughly speaking, by rotating people through the dull, routine jobs and allowing those able to practise the more incremental ones to find the variety they need within the exercise of their specific set of skill and powers. Doctors could find the variety they needed in their medical practice; others could shift employment.

One can easily form a concrete picture of a society in which there was less conflict between the desire for varied activity and the need for routine work than we think. I actually rather enjoyed the six weeks during the summer which I spent scrubbing the walls and floors of the canteen in the steel mill, because it was different from what I usually spent my time doing during the rest of the year (reading Greek texts, going to lectures, writing essays). During the first week or two I was able to learn some techniques for working more efficiently at the tasks I had to perform.

Furthermore, as a result of a number of different accidental factors, such as the fact that the US economy as a whole was booming, the steel mill had a strong labour union (it was a 'closed shop', meaning that employment was conditional on joining the United Steel Workers' Union), and there was a temporary local labour shortage, the job was adequately, if not opulently, paid – relative to what were at the time my relatively simple needs (I was young) and the general cost of living at the time on the east coast of the United States. Finally, because I was not trapped in that job for life, I could integrate it into various of my larger projects, especially that of understanding the world in which I was living. I would happily have gone back to that job for a few weeks at a time once a year or so, if necessary, but I would not, of course, have been happy to have had no choice but to stay in it full-time for thirty years.

The Economics of 'I and We'

When anyone asks the question 'who is working?,' there are always two answers to that question: first 'I am' and second 'we are'. Both of them need to be taken into account; to leave either one of them untreated is to neglect something important. In working I am always embedded in a collaborative context with others, and outside that context what I do is usually both physically impossible and makes no sense. This is obvious in cases like agriculture or industry, where there are tasks that require the cooperation of more than one person, but it is true even of more abstract activities such as writing a book. Who ever wrote a book without discussing any of its topics with any other person? The collaboration inherent in work is not restricted to the present, but also has a historical dimension. When my uncle worked his farm, the 'we' who were harvesting the field in some not insignificant sense included the men who had built his combine harvester.

Shades of Descartes, Shades of Locke (in the Economy)

This view will seem counterintuitive to people who have grown up in societies like ours, where common sense is deeply informed by a set of assumptions about the radical priority of the 'I'. Surely, one is inclined to say, it can't be right to suggest that there is anything like equal validity to both these ways of looking at work – 'I am working' and 'We are working.' Surely no one thinks these two can have equal weight. 'I am working' expresses something real, palpable, and irreducible. Compared with the overwhelming self-evidence of this reality, any purported 'we'-perspective is a mere artificial construct, an abstract and intangible afterthought. When, in one of my industrial jobs, I burned one of my arms on a coil of very hot steel which I accidentally brushed up against, it was *my* arm that was burned, not one of the phantom limbs of some purported 'we, the workers in US Steel'.

The common-sense view about the automatic priority of the 'I', which I am repudiating, is constructed from a collection of debased recollections of Descartes and Locke. It starts from the idea that the 'I' (or the 'me') is something absolutely basic and fundamental. Its ontological status is unclear (in this, then, departing from the historical Descartes who thought that this status was not unclear, but was that of a 'substance') – maybe it is not a substance or a thing or a property of a thing, but just some kind of psychic unity or reflective function – but the details of this are unimportant. Whatever it is, it is immediately accessible to me in introspection and what I find there is, if not absolutely certain, at least practically undeniable. 'I know what I think and want': what could be clearer or more certain than that? This undeniable locus of me-ness may then engage with the world in various ways. One way in which it may do that is by working, say cultivating a strip of land and making it into a garden. In working I am 'mixing my labour' with the earth, and, by so doing (now comes the vague recollection of something Locke might have said) I acquire ownership of it and make it my property[14] (provided no one else already owns it). By working on it – always provided no one has a prior claim to it – I acquire a right to it and what it produces, and this right does not depend on 'the assignation or con-sent of any body'. This utterly pre-social, pre-political fact of the connection of my self-referential 'I' through work to *this* bit of external reality is the firm foundation on which all the shifting superstructures of our social and cultural life and our politics are built.

Unfortunately, some may recall that in the passage from Locke on which the last part of the above is vaguely based, Locke says more exactly that he has a right to that with which he has mixed his labour, including what he has himself sweated over and what he has dug out of the earth. He also claims the same right to 'the turfs my servant has cut'. How exactly does the servant's labour give Locke a right to these turfs? Is it plausible that Locke's relation to his servant, a relation that gives him the right to what the servant finds, grows, or produces, is completely pre-social and pre-political, and based on no 'assignation or consent of any body'?

'The Appropriative I'

Locke's claim to ownership of the 'turfs my servant has cut' is an instance of a phenomenon which I call 'the appropriative I', and which came to my attention when for the first time in my life I met a real banker. I was struck by the way in which he would say 'I won't lend my money to X.' I understood immediately that he did not mean he was refusing to put his hand into his pocket to withdraw some notes and coins for X. Neither did he mean that he was going to assign some money from his own bank account to X. What he meant was that he was refusing to assign to X money which *other people* had deposited in the bank he worked for. By 'my money' he certainly did not mean anything he had earned by the sweat of his own brow, or inherited from his frugal and diligent grandfather, or even an entitlement to own something which he had himself acquired by activity in the fields of commerce and finance. What he meant was that other people had deposited money in the bank where he worked, he had worked his way up the hierarchy of employees in the bank, and he could now extend his 'I/my' sphere to include the money deposited and could treat it as 'his' for purposes of lending or refusing to lend.

Similarly, Locke, who was himself an investor in the slave trade, could easily imagine his 'I' expanding to encompass what the servant did and the results of what his servant did. Think of him addressing one of his servants: '*We* need turf, so *you* must go and cut *me* some.' The differential extensions of his 'I' and of his servant's 'I' would have seemed perfectly natural to him: 'What *you* cut is yours, therefore *ours*, therefore *mine* (although what is *mine* is not necessarily *ours* to share, and certainly not *yours*).' To be a servant was to learn corresponding imaginative tricks: 'the turf I cut => the Master's turf; my theft of a loaf of bread => my hanging'. In this passage Locke also shows himself in an unwonted guise, as a precursor of Jarry, Ionesco, and Beckett, when he imagines that his 'I' can be expanded to encompass not just the turfs which his 'servant' cuts, but 'the grass my horse has bit'.

The appropriative I is a bit like a modern variant of the old-fashioned royal 'we'. Brecht made the basic point about it with his usual pithiness when he wrote

> The young Alexander conquered India.
> All by himself?
> Caesar defeated the Gauls
> Did he not have even a cook
> with him?[15]

Edifying and Less Edifying Variants

Much of the attraction of the view that connects property with work (often via some notion of 'desert') derives from thinking about a particular set of overly simplified and ahistorical examples. Surely, many people would argue, the farmer who has successfully cultivated his fields by the sweat of his brow for decades has *some* claim on being allowed to continue working them, if he wishes, and on not being forcibly evicted for no good reason at all. Of course, the use of the term 'evict' already shows that this example is one imagined as taking place not in a pre-social state, but in a society having something like the rules of property which we have. Also one has to ask whether anyone was on the land before the farmer and what happened to those who were there. The example of the North American pioneer family looks slightly different if one thinks that the land became available for cultivation when the existing indigenous population was physically exterminated. In addition, the pioneer model is a very implausible account of how fortunes are actually made now. A multimillionaire media entrepreneur may well have earned his position and wealth by working very hard. What if this work consisted partly in noticing and snapping up a technical invention made by a researcher at a publicly funded university, but mostly in adroit financial transactions, sharp practice with suppliers, and ruthlessly marginalising, damaging, and eliminating possible competitors (whose technology was just as good) so that he could establish a de facto monopoly in his particular domain?

How the results and proceeds of what 'we' do ('we' the farm family, the European settlers, the workers in steel mills over the generations, the depositors and investors in banks, the technicians and marketers of internet companies) get assigned to individuals is always a matter of politics. There is no natural, completely pre-political chain of causality which one can follow and which will of itself give an answer to the question of who should receive what. The decisions that have in fact been made about who gets what result from a variety of factors which I will list in more or less decreasing order of importance: the use of sheer force (no Native Americans left on the ground to dispute claims), historical accident (inheritance), complex political manipulations, negotiations, and a very thin sprinkling of appeals to a variety of moral sentiments ('this is merited; that would be cruel, indecent, unjust/unfair'). There is no reason to believe that the complex web of moral sentiments that structure what we think is merited, deserved, just, fair, humane, and so on can be reduced to some single dimension, and no reason to think that even if that were the case, any theory about that single dimension would have much real effect on the world. There is certainly no natural or irresistibly rational path that leads from work to remuneration. 'I' is not an aboriginal *fundamentum inconcussum* but a position in a complex game of 'I, you, we, and they' – a game which we learn before anything else, which is always already in progress, and which is the foundation of anything we can accomplish. The particular terms on which the game is played are, however, highly variable, open-ended, and subject to revision.

Since, at the very latest, the time of Rimbaud and Nietzsche,[16] we have come to realise that contrary to what Descartes suggests, the 'I' is not a given, but is just as much a construct of the imagination as the 'we' is. Similarly, we are well aware that 'my servant' has as its necessary correlate 'my master'. What holds that relation together can only be expressed in a very idiosyncratic set of rules for determining who is allowed to extend and who must restrict the 'I'; how far, under which circumstances, the extension is permitted to go; who is permitted, under what circumstances, to be part of the 'we', who is forced to join 'us', and who is radically excluded.

4 Radical Discontent and the Future of Work

Forms of Radical Discontent

Dissatisfaction with work is as old as work itself, and dissatisfaction with our regime of work is as old as industrialism itself. Sometimes complaints about work are very well focused, such as the complaints made by health-workers in the British National Health Service (NHS) during the COVID-19 pandemic of 2020 that they were not provided with appropriate protective equipment despite the fact that one of the government's own exercises had highlighted this as an area of potential concern during a pandemic. Sometimes, however, the discontent is of a kind that cannot be addressed by a mere tweaking of current arrangements, and it expresses itself in more radical demands. In what follows I shall discuss some frequently made suggestions for making radical changes to our world of work.

Simple Abolition of Work

The first kind of dissatisfaction can be seen to be peeping out from behind such phenomena as the persistent fantasy of the land of Cockaigne, a place of such natural plenty that life is easy and work superfluous. In fact, of course, work has been increasingly mechanised for centuries. Even Homer (*Iliad* 18, 370ff.) describes the self-moving (*automata*)

115

mechanical assistants which the god Hephaistos has created to help him work his forge. What is more natural than simply to continue in this direction and project a possible state of our world in which human work is completely abolished? This would be a world in which, say, self-moving harvesters brought in crops and self-regulating robots worked in the factories.

Thinking about the purported utopia of Cockaigne in a sustained way, however, tends to bring out dystopian elements of this conception as well. I'll mention just four of these.

The first thing to note here is, to recur to Dewey's point mentioned in the previous chapter (p. 100), the extreme insipidity of a life completely without exertion, difficulties, or obstacles. As has often been observed, Dante's *Inferno* is more interesting than his *Paradiso*, and many traditional conceptions of heaven as a 'Sabbath of Sabbaths' make it seem distinctly boring. Cockaigne, or a permanent Super-Sabbath, may seem an attractive compensatory fantasy to peasants who work from sun-up to sundown in the fields, but its attraction is mostly derived precisely from that status as a *contrast* to reality. If that reality no longer existed, the imaginary construct would suddenly be seen to be deeply unappealing, not just uninteresting but intolerable, even for a peasant who remembered what it had been like to work. Life there would be *senseless* because the meaningful structure of a human life is a micro-weave of tiny episodes of encountering and overcoming obstacles, and if this is completely abolished, what exactly could be the point of what is left? The only possible state for a human in which there was no friction, no obstacles, and no need for exertion would be death. One can take Nirvana to be the ultimate form of bliss if one wishes, and many have, but there is no passion, desire, disappointment, frustration, triumph, or failure in Nirvana. That is one of the reasons why it seems so attractive to many, but also why it is not a good model for understanding human life and a hopeless one for understanding human society.

A second dystopian variant on this theme is the subject of E. M. Forster's story 'The Machine Stops'. Surely part of the intent behind the fantasy of 'complete' mechanisation is that we no longer have to keep practising the skills we would need to be able to survive without machines, or even the skills necessary to supervise and maintain them. What then happens if something goes wrong with the machines, for instance if they run out of energy or otherwise simply stop? Are we willing to trust that their auto-learning programmes will allow them to deal with the radically unexpected?

If the fear in this case is that the machines won't work, or won't be able to adapt to the unexpected, or will eventually wear out, the third dystopian fantasy starts in a way from the opposite assumption. The machines become all too good at functioning, coping, learning, and evolving. Part of this would be that they learn to take independent decisions and generate new goals, something one might think is essential if they are to respond to new situations. If they function perfectly and begin to pursue new goals, how do we know that their goals will not be different from, or even incompatible with, ours, or, for that matter, that they will have any positive interest at all in our continued existence? Mary Shelley's *Frankenstein* is not about mechanisation but about, we might now say, biotechnology, but the fear which it expresses about a human technical creation which makes itself independent and develops into a threat to its own creator is the start of a whole genre of similar cautionary tales.

The fourth case is somewhat more subtle than these first three cases. People in the land of Cockaigne would seem almost inevitably to be bored, but something further is also likely to be true about them. Toward the end of the *ancien régime* in the late eighteenth century the Encyclopedist Denis Diderot wrote his remarkable novel *Jacques le fataliste*. The novel's narrative concerns a master and his servant, a factotum named Jacques, who are on a trip the object of which is unclear until the very end of the novel; the trip is interrupted by a series of highly contingent events that unexpectedly intervene and are the occasion for a long series of individual stories told by Jacques about his life. One of the most striking features of this novel is that it is Jacques, the servant, who is really the centre of attention. He is the one who engages with the world and takes care that things actually get done, and he is by far the most interesting character. By comparison with him, the Master is a complete cipher; he doesn't even have a proper name, just going by 'the Master'. As Hegel says about him, his only activity is taking snuff, asking what time it is, and listening to Jacques recount his many adventures. The Master's complete failure to engage with the world of necessary work leads to a deep unseriousness of character. This is not like the *ennui* which affects people in Cockaigne, because it is not that the Master is described as particularly bored. In a way he is too empty-headed to be bored. He is *boring* because he has nothing to say for himself. He has become an irremediably lightweight person whose life seems totally inconsequential. This is not a case in which all the work is done by machines, rather one person does all the work for someone else, but there is every reason to believe that the implication would still hold in a fully mechanised world. Would a world of complex machines that did all the work not naturally create a population of shallow, simple-minded people?

Hegel was an avid and attentive reader of Diderot, and he explicitly and systematically draws what he takes to be the proper conclusions from the description of Jacques and the Master, expressing them in his own rather abstract and peculiar idiom. Hegel essentially construes the Master in his pure form as a representative of the '*noblesse d'épée*' of the *ancien régime* whose main raison d'être was his military prowess: in particular the great courage he exhibits (or once exhibited) in risking his life in armed combat. This, the Master holds, gives him a right to the enjoyment of what is his, including the exploitation of the full labour-power of the servant (who is presumed to have originally been a war-captive). If, however, the servant really does all the work, he at least has a chance of learning to develop and control his own powers in this process. If the Master really does nothing but merely enjoy what the servant prepares for him, it is the

Master who will quickly become an irrelevant nullity. The Masters may appropriate and consume the bread, the wine, and the game, but it is the servants who will become expert bakers and viticulturalists, who will get to know the habits of the game and how to capture them, and who will (have to) learn to turn their hand to a variety of tasks in order to be able to do whatever the Masters wish. It is through work that the servant becomes serious, learns about the real world, gains skills, and thus acquires a potentially rich and articulated inner life.

So the ideal Master, in this Hegelian construct, reserves for himself pure enjoyment, while delegating to the servant all the work; consequently it is the servant who will acquire distinct skills, knowledge of the world, and forms of self-control. Marx adds to this that Masters, if they really become nothing but consumption-machines, will eventually even fail to 'enjoy correctly', because enjoyment is itself a human skill or power that can and must be cultivated, and its cultivation must in some way be connected with being seriously active, and eventually with the activity of work.[1] The enjoyment of the Masters will not merely be 'pure' but will also be crude. Their much-vaunted courage, their willingness to risk their lives and face death, is perfectly real, but it becomes socially and in other respects irrelevant. The virtue of courage alone is a dead-end. Nothing follows from the momentary gesture of defiance of death made by such an empty-headed creature of enjoyment. As Hegel says in a slightly different context, the death of such a Master is nothing more significant than the lopping-off of a head of cabbage.[2]

Overcoming Alienation

Thinkers in the Hegelian tradition do not really wish to have any truck with proposals that amount to the complete abolition of strenuous exercise in the production of things necessary to life and to the performance of essential services. However, there was a slightly different line about the discontents of labour that many of them did pursue. Perhaps the most widely canvassed of these and the one that has had the most historical traction is one developed by Marx in the 1840s, which starts from the (originally Hegelian) concept of 'alienation'.[3] The Hegelian concept is very general in its scope: Y is 'alienated' from X, if Y ought really (in some sense) to belong to X, but does not. Looking at it from the point of view of X: Y 'ought' to be 'mine' but is not. What 'mine' means (and what 'belongs to' means in the previous formula) is open to interpretation. If a general before a battle has three army corps (I, II, and III) and just as the battle begins, Corps III goes over to the enemy, that corps has been alienated (or has alienated itself): the general had reason to think Corps III was 'his', but now it is 'theirs'. Similarly, if you steal my pen from my pocket, you have 'alienated' it: it ought to be 'mine' but now it is not. If a subordinate works out in detail a plan, and this is presented by one of her male superiors as his own plan, he has 'alienated' it. Suppose that a sporting team, 'Dynamo Axxa', has for decades been located in the city of Axxa; the townsfolk of Axxa have supported and fostered the team over the years in a number of ways, and it is a matter of no little local pride. The inhabitants of Axxa think of the members of the team as very much '*nashi*' ('our boys'). Then the team is sold and physically moved to the city Bexxa (which is a long way from Axxa) and has its name changed to 'Dynamo Bexxa'. Suppose now that the newly constituted 'Dynamo Bexxa' roundly defeats a succession of scratch teams that the town of Axxa is able to field against them. The members of 'Dynamo Bexxa' remain the same (for a while at least) as those of 'Dynamo Axxa' were, but the team has been 'alienated' from its fans and supporters in Axxa.

Marx uses 'alienation' in three contexts. The first two are religion and politics. Religion is a realm of alienation because the 'God' of theism is an imaginary projection of what are in fact our own human powers, writ large and ascribed to a being conceived to be radically 'other'. The usual kind of politics is a form of alienation because it is about state power, and 'the state' is a structure in which our own powers have made themselves independent of our control and oppress us. The third form of alienation which Marx discusses is the one which will now occupy us, alienation of labour. Recall Hegel's example of the little boy throwing rocks into the pool. The sphere of work, that is the activity of producing some discernible external effect on the world, ought to be a domain in which I create meaning by expressing and affirming myself. As such I should see my own activity there, and the products of that activity, as fundamentally under my own control. However, Marx's observation of industrial work in the nineteenth century led him to the conclusion that it was impossible to instantiate anything like this model under the economic conditions then dominant. The factory-owners, not the workers, owned the product produced and the machines used for production, and had the power to control the conditions under which production took place. They used this power ruthlessly to try to further their own interests. These interests (low wages, minimal safety precautions, long hours) were, however, in fact completely different from those of the workers. Given the difference in power between the owners and the workers, the owners were able to see to it that their interests took priority in cases of conflict, cases which were, given the form of economic organisation in question, systemic. In these circumstances the whole sphere of work was a domain in which workers were 'alienated': something that should be expressive of them and under their control, a sphere in which they should affirm themselves and be able to create meaning, had made itself completely independent of them and in fact controlled and subjugated them; it confronted them as something alien to their interests.

People now frequently use the expression 'I feel alienated', and so for this reason it might seem natural to us to construe alienation as a particular state of individual psychic distress. For Marx, however, alienation is not in the first instance a concept in individual psychology. It refers to a real state of affairs, an ontological condition – that is, the worker is alienated not because she *experiences* a loss of meaning or *feels* as if her work life is out of her control or *views herself* as separated from her product. Rather, she is alienated because she actually *is* separated from her product – which belongs to the factory-owner and at the end of the work process will be taken away and sold in ways over which she has no control, in order to generate profits which the factory-owner will appropriate. Given that she actually *has* no control, it will not be odd that she also comes to realise that she has no control, and this realisation could be expected to have various concomitant psychological effects (rage, depression, etc.). However, the alienation is the fact of lack of control, not the psychic, emotional, or attitudinal reaction to it. In fact, it is possible for workers to *be* alienated without realising it or having any particular negative attitudinal reaction to it. That is, in a way, a state of the greatest perversion – my life is meaningless *and I don't even realise it* – and a state that the factory-owners will have a keen interest in promoting because it can be expected to make the work-force more biddable.

Still, one might think that the whole project of 'overcoming alienation' was doomed from the start. Why should I initially be at all inclined to think as I look around at the machines in the factory that all of this, and all that I produce with it, 'ought' to be mine? The model of the Hegelian little boy throwing the stone into the pool is misleading. Even to suggest that the whole of his 'product', the result of his action, is fully under his control is false, because the effects are partly a natural phenomenon. If he wanted to produce square ripples on the water, he would be completely out of luck. He does something, and what he does is to some extent under his control, but the result will certainly not be fully under his control. That is the stubborn objectivity of nature which we will never be able to over-come or abolish, and which will prevent us from ever iden-tifying completely with the results of any of our actions. Second, the little boy is an individual throwing one natural object, a stone, into another, a pool, and the example has been constructed in such a way that the possible social context does not seem relevant, but work processes, certainly work processes of any complexity in the modern world, are not at all like that. The machines that surround me in the factory are not like stones lying on the ground, waiting to be picked up. They were created by others for their own purposes; why assume that I can simply appropriate them for my own use and then use them successfully for my self-affirmation? They may be structured around completely different goals. Why must I be able to find my self-expression in the machines provided by previous generations of workers who collectively produced this set of tools for the making and forging of steel?

As far as the second of these questions is concerned, it is, of course, correct that Hegel's example presents in the form of a rudimentary fairy tale what is an abstract individual action, for which the social context is not directly relevant. Work, certainly work in the modern world, is not at all like that, but is rather an inherently social or collective process. The worker in a factory works *as part of a group*. As such, there can be no question of such an individual worker finding purely individual self-expression *outside* the collective action of a working 'we'. It is in the first instance 'we, the workers of this factory' who act, and then 'we, the workers of the world' who must be seen as acting through history to put our imprint on the world, inventing and deploying machines of various kinds in the course of that history. Any individual can come to have control over the productive process as a whole, *only* as an (appropriately integrated) member of the group of workers as a whole. This resolves part of the problem but only at the cost of generating another one. Now the exact meanings of 'we' and of 'appropriately integrated' become crucial. How do we all have to be related to each other in working so that we form an appropriate 'we', that is, so that each of us is able to identify with the whole of the activity and the resulting whole product?

So the framework for thinking about work and alienation is one of an open-ended group, as a 'we' (composed of individuals who can say 'I') who are collectively producing. This still does not deal with the unavoidable recalcitrance of nature to the human will (individual or collective). Even organised as a coherent collective working subject, we can't be sure nature will be at all amenable to our efforts; even the whole human species appropriately organised as a 'we' cannot be sure that when we throw the stone into the pool, the ripples will be square. Even if we could abolish untransparent 'social necessity' in our organisation of work – the need for the profit of the enterprise to be above $x\%$ – there would still remain a certain natural necessity which we would have to confront, and we would not be confronting it realistically if we simply pretended it did not exist.

So, for the project of completely abolishing alienation to be sensible, one would have to be able to make a relatively clear distinction between three things:

(a) 'social necessities' that were mere pseudo-necessities imposed by what are in principle variable forms of the organisation of labour, for instance, according to Marx, in our society the 'necessity' that work be organised in such a way that invested capital can make (what it takes to be appropriate) profits

(b) 'real necessities of the social organisation of work', for instance that it takes the coordinated action of two workers to operate a two-person saw, or to move a girder of a certain size and weight

(c) real natural necessities, such as that ore must be fired to a certain temperature in order to make iron.

Stage (b) constitutes something distinctive and different from stage (c) because the temperature at which iron ore changes its state is invariant in all societies, whereas the two-person saw is a particular social creation: it represents a certain level of technological development, so the necessity to have two people to operate it is relative to the existence of that level of development. Capitalism battens on the difficulty in distinguishing exactly what features of the work process belong in (a) above and what belong in (b). Marx's idea is that (a) can be abolished and that (b) will then, or can then be made to, map or track (c). Short of commitment to a full form of idealism, though, it still seems unclear how in this scheme the residual resistance of the world to our will can be completely overcome. Nevertheless, as socially necessary forms of alienation decrease and control over nature increases, Marx seems to think that nature itself will come to seem less and less 'alien' to us. Unfortunately, an integral part of this conception is a kind of productivism: an ideal of the progressive instrumental mastery of the natural world in the interests of producing ever more objects. Human history is taken to be that of the progressive development of our productive powers, of ever-increasing actual production and of ever more sophisticated manipulation of nature. The future is to be more of the same, with human productive powers fully unleashed and developed for their own sake and 'not measured according to any pre-existing measure'.[4]

Non-instrumental Care

It is in reaction to this image of human productive work gone out of control, in a world that is increasingly being forced to confront the ecological limits to unfettered growth, that some thinkers have taken a different tack from that of Hegel and Marx and have tried to argue for a return to a pastoral model of human engagement with nature in general and of human work in particular. The advocacy of a pastoralist ethos is particularly strongly associated with the writings of the philosopher Martin Heidegger, who developed views in this direction in the 1940s and increasingly toward the end of his career. Heidegger thinks that we in the West have come to believe that humans have a vocation to get likenesses of the things in the world. Originally these likenesses were sought in the form of images or pictures, and then eventually in the form of concepts, which are a kind of picture-derivative. Through a long and confusing set of historical steps, we also came to develop the idea of 'truth' and imposed on ourselves the demand that the images/concepts of the world we formed were to be 'true'. 'Truth' was increasingly misconceived as something instrumental. This meant that gradually the concepts and the theories which we developed about the world based on such concepts became tools for manipulating our environment. A manipulative attitude is inherent in Western culture since the early Greeks and, in particular, it is implicit in all our conceptual thought, especially scientific thought. This is an extremely bald and condensed summary of what is a tremendously long and complicated story and one which is recounted by Heidegger in great detail in his many scattered works on the history of philosophy. He thinks we must try to start thinking about the world again in a non-instrumental way, and recommends a kind of pastoralism as the appropriate life-context for this new way of thinking.

Actually there are three strands in the late Heidegger's thought. First, there is pastoralism per se. Heidegger speaks of humanity as needing to become not a Maker of Images of Being (even if these are conceptual, not visual), or the Master of Nature, but its shepherd (*Hirt des Seins*).[5] Even agriculture is too invasive and too 'terrible' (*deinon*): the plough itself is a violation of Mother Nature,[6] presumably because it manipulates her instead of cherishing her. Instead of conceptualising nature, speaking about it, working on it, and intervening in it or even violating it, we should try to learn to care for it, cultivate it, and foster it. The second strand is a specific further interpretation of what that 'care' means. It is *not* a kind of non-instrumental but active tending, but rather it is what Heidegger calls *Gelassenheit*, a relaxed detachment or letting things take their course.[7] Even, presumably, Adam's prelapsarian horti-cultural work in the garden of Eden and Voltaire's advice '*il faut cultiver son jardin*'[8] are still too much like intervention to be an instance of what Heidegger has in mind. Third,

Heidegger thinks that attaining *Gelassenheit* and breaking with a basically manipulative attitude toward the world can be successful only if one also escapes from 'the history of metaphysics' and finds a way of thinking which is a-conceptual and thus completely different from our present forms of science. The later Heidegger himself looked to poetry, especially (but not exclusively) the kind of vatic poetry represented by, for instance, Hölderlin, Rilke, and Trakl, to find an alternative non-conceptual way of thinking and speaking, but basically no one has a real idea of what an appropriate non-conceptualism would look like. There was a long tradition of thought in Central Europe, most strongly represented perhaps by the Romantics and by some philosophers who were influenced by them, which sought (in one way or another) to dethrone conceptual thought in favour of a revitalisation of myth. This line of thinking had some perfectly respectable supporters in the nineteenth century, but it came to be pretty thoroughly discredited by its association with European Fascism in the 1930s and 1940s. Heidegger does not specifically endorse 'myth' as what he is looking for, but that is probably because he thinks that 'myth' is inherently defined by what it is contrasted with (namely, *logos*/reason/the concept), and he thinks you will only really get beyond the concept if you also get beyond something inherently defined in opposition to it. That is all fair enough, but still leaves us at an impasse with no idea how to proceed.

We might think that we could (and should) stop at the first of Heidegger's three points; we can replace the Stakhanovite worker with the shepherd as the model of the way in which we satisfy our basic needs and maintain ourselves in existence. Surely, we might think, it would be enough to replace ruthless exploitation of nature through work with something more horticultural or pastoral, less brutal and violent, more circumspect, more concerned with the integrity of nature and naturally existing forms of harmony. We would have to get rid of the part of the usual pastoralist ideology which advocates trying infinitely to increase one's flocks, but why should it be impossible to dispense with that?

Trying to do this, of course, immediately leads us back to the discussion between Socrates and Thrasymachus (p. 66). Does the shepherd care for the sheep for the sheep's benefit or (finally) for his own? It might make sense to have an 'ethics of care' in our relation to other people because we assume that they have interests, preferences, views, opinions, and reactions much like ours, and we can learn to take account of these, try to understand them, accommodate them, and so on. Maybe I can even try to adopt the point of view of the sheep and imagine what they would want, what opinions they would have, what courses of action they would adopt if free. In fact, of course, we do this all the time in our interaction with animals. This requires a bit of an imaginative stretch sometimes, but so much the better. However, in tending our own garden, we seem to have gone beyond anything that could be construed in these terms. It may be *both* in my interest and in (what I conceive to be) the sheep's interest that he go to the sheep dip today, but what interests do my roses have? Is a tropical forest more 'natural' than a desert? Is a hectare of land which supports a certain number of separate species of plants and animals more 'natural' than one that supports three times that many? Unfortunately, a preference for biodiversity, as far as I can tell, is a human, and highly anthropocentric, value-judgement, related either to a vague idea that having greater biodiversity will (eventually) be of some use to us (for medicinal plants) or to some of our aesthetic preferences (we prefer wild growth to monoculture or scorched earth). 'Nature' herself, however, does not prefer to be diverse (or to be uniform and homogeneous). Perhaps the problem is the very personification of 'nature', but if we get rid of all personification in this domain – all appeals to what 'nature herself wants' – it seems that we are back in the fully depersonalised world of technological manipulation, which is what we wanted to get out of in the first place. 'Care for nature' means care for us and for the related species of animals with which we can imaginatively identify to an appropriately high degree. We may be able to assume that the cat would prefer not to have fleas, but it is *we* who prefer the rose to the mildew spore, not the rose.[9]

It is, then, fair enough to say that we should take a broad and long view of our own interests and preferences rather than a narrower one. It is better *for us* (in the long run) not to poison the environment and to maintain as much biodiversity as possible. This is certainly very good advice, and not something that self-evidently requires a revolution in metaphysics rather than a certain number of political, economic, legal, and social changes to the way we live.

The Future of Work

To predict the future of work is both completely impossible and utterly unavoidable. How can we *not* allow much of our action to be informed by some (at best sketchy) ideas about the future, even though we know that this future will never turn out exactly as we imagined? If, however, we always in fact presuppose at least some vague idea of what the future will hold, then we have no choice but to try to form the conceptions we have of possible futures as carefully as we can. The alternative, as historical experience has shown, is to allow ourselves to remain at best clueless, which in effect means being guided by some completely unreflective set of prejudices, or at worst wilfully self-deluded.

What follows in this section should not be construed as a prediction, a kind of crystal ball-gazing. It is rather just an attempt to sensitise us to some dimensions which seem at the moment to be potentially problematic and to which we think it important to pay attention. This does not mean that we cannot *still* be surprised by events that could not have been predicted.

So what trends are discernible in work at the present time (the 2020s)? The first is not really a trend, but rather a structural change in the social context within which work in most Western societies takes place. This is the development in most advanced Western countries of some provision for the welfare of those who must work for a living. The existence of disability insurance, unemployment benefits, governmentally underwritten pension schemes, and (at least in many countries) universal health care (such as that provided by the National Health Service in Britain) has significantly changed the environment within which work takes place, partly by modifying the relevant notion of the 'necessity' of work. The disabled, infirm, or unemployed don't routinely and quickly starve to death. This is deplored by a small number of ideologues, but by most people it is considered to be a form of social progress. It does, however, have the effect that the sense of complete urgency that accompanied everything associated with work for the traditional industrial worker is somewhat softened around the edges. This cannot be totally without consequences for the role which work plays in our lives.

Automation and Precariousness

The first thing that is noticeable in the contemporary world of work is that the historical trend toward automation has continued and accelerated. Historically, humans lifting and moving burdens themselves are eventually replaced by self-driving, self-unloading machines. The tens of thousands of dock-workers and longshoremen are replaced by hundreds of operators of cranes and fork-lifts. One obvious consequence of this is mass unemployment. The idea that for every docker's job abolished, another job as a crane-operator or logistics engineer is created is baseless. For an individual firm it would seem obvious: why install new automated processes that abolish the relatively low-paid jobs of thousands, if one then has to hire the same number of more highly paid technicians and operators? If one looks at employment not from the point of view of one particular enterprise, but globally, the picture is the same: a few, highly qualified jobs will be created by automation, but these amount to a small fraction of the number of those made redundant. Or rather, the result of the continuing historical process of automation is the separation of the previous work-force into three parts. The largest part consists simply of those who have become unemployed and potentially unemployable – such as the 1.5 million lorry, coach, fork-lift, and taxi drivers who will become redundant in Britain when all vehicular traffic is automated, as may soon be the case. Second, there will be a small remaining work-force retained for jobs that it is not yet technically possible or economically feasible to abolish, say a couple of thousand people to service self-driving cars: these people will be subject to working conditions of increasing and withering stress. Finally, there may be a tiny number, say a few hundred, of new jobs that might be created, or existing jobs slightly enhanced and upgraded, such as people to programme traffic.

When we think of automation, we tend to think of it as a simple extension of old-style mechanisation, that is, the replacement of human muscle power by the actions of an automated system. A further aspect of the same process, though, is the application of all the techniques of social scientific research, especially what used to be called 'time-and-motion' studies or 'efficiency studies', to subject the workers who remain in employment, my second category above, to a ruthless work discipline. It is now possible to use scientific techniques to determine, for many of the remaining tasks for which people are employed, exactly what is the minimum time in which any specific task can be accomplished, and surveillance techniques mean that one can control even the smallest details of the work process and intensify it up to the very limits of what is humanly possible. Not only does the worker lose control of the total number of hours which she works, and general control over what tasks are assigned to her, but she loses completely control over the level of intensity of work in any period and the rhythm of what she is doing.

One can track this gradual loss of control by imagining it as proceeding through three steps. Consider first the description that George Orwell gave in his book *Down and Out in Paris and London* of working as a *plongeur* (a member of the kitchen staff) in the 1930s in a large Parisian hotel. The kitchen staff had no control over the absolute amount of their work and, as a general rule, always had too much to do. Since the *patron* (understandably) insisted that every client be served in a reasonable amount of time, how much work there was to do at any one time depended on who came into the restaurant when. The work, however, was in fact concentrated in two peak periods: a lunch period and a dinner period. In the middle of the afternoon, after the lunch hour and before dinner, there was a slight reduction in intensity, in fact a pause in the work routine. The workers were even able to relax slightly. In addition, the *plongeurs* turned the very extremity of pressure which they were subject to, and their own ability to manage it, into a matter of pride: they were '*durs*'; they were *débrouillards*, 'hard' people who could cope with anything that could be thrown at them. The management of the restaurant could, of course, sack any *plongeur* at any time, especially if they could not keep up with the work, but as long as they did keep up, the *patron* had no interest in *how* they worked. This was a brutal, but also oddly humane, system compared with some of the things that have come later.

Now take, as the second case, the work of a chambermaid in a large hotel today. The hotel management has highly precise conceptions of exactly how each room must be made up – how the beds are to be made, how many towels there will be on the towel rack, how any objects on the tables are to be stacked or arranged – and they have employed scientific experts to conduct extensive time-and-motion studies to determine exactly how many rooms an employee can make up to a given standard in, say, an hour. If a chambermaid fails to make up the prescribed number of rooms in a given hour to the specified standard, she is fired immediately. Here the amount of work is set in a way over which the worker has no control. It has nothing to do with the number of actual guests in the hotel; there is no more intense and no less intense period of work, and the tempo at which it is performed is also completely out of the worker's control too. It must be, say, six rooms per hour.

The third case is a form of work which is now just being developed, but will very soon be upon us. In 2018 Amazon took out patents on two devices that can go on a wristband and can track every movement of the hand on which it is strapped.[10] This hyper-fine-tuned tracking apparatus permits a kind of surveillance literally of every gesture of every worker, control beyond the wildest dreams of the *patron* of Orwell's Parisian hotel. The devices make even the smallest motion discernible, so that it becomes possible to envisage a calculated intensification of every aspect of the work process in the interests of greater profitability. The surveillance means that the individual worker loses control not just over the absolute amount of work, and the general division of it into periods, but even over individual movements of the hand. As far as anyone knows, these wristbands are not (yet) capable of administering electric shocks. It is unlikely that workers will develop even the slightly perverse pride which *plongeurs* take in their work, if they have to work under these conditions.

As the scientifically calculated pressure on the chambermaid's job is intensified, her pay is, naturally, not increased, although the increase in her efficiency will allow the hotel to reduce its costs by reducing its staff. If ten chambermaids can be made to do the job for which twelve used to be needed, two will be fired and the work they used to do redistributed among the ten who are retained. So both forms of automation – the direct introduction of new machines, and the intensification of the work routines resulting from the application of results obtained by using the techniques of behavioural scientific research – will have the effect of allowing the enterprise in question to shed jobs.

It has also been widely noted that employment in the contemporary world has become particularly precarious. Although the state provides some support for those without employment, it has become much easier to lose one's job. In one sense, of course, jobs have always been precarious. The Anatolian agriculturist in the sixth century BC could not be sure that he would continue to be harvesting the same fields in two years' time because he could not be sure that he would not be dead, and dead men have no jobs. Similarly, it is hard to think of industrial jobs in the nineteenth century as being anything other than precarious for the workers involved. Those workers were regularly vulnerable to virtually arbitrary dismissal by particular employers in addition to being subject to the usual systemic economic threats associated with the 'business cycle'. What is perhaps true is that what used to be perceived as steady, middle-class jobs are now becoming as precarious as industrial employment was. Instead of (at least potentially) being permanent jobs, even white-collar work is becoming increasingly temporary and part-time, or otherwise irregular.

This trend is visible even in sectors like the universities, where people in permanent posts are being transformed into a tiny elite who are encouraged to engage in the constant pursuit of grants and the creation of high-visibility special projects, while more and more of the actual teaching is delegated to badly paid part-time staff who are overworked and have no job security whatever. This is part of a general development which Marx foresaw when he predicted the eventual proletarianisation of middle-class forms of employment. Obviously, any kind of job stability or security was always directly incompatible with one of the much noted, and – by some theorists at least – also much celebrated, features of our economic system, namely that it was based on continuous creative destruction, but the panegyrists of creative destruction always assumed that as old jobs were destroyed, an equal number of well-paid jobs with good working conditions would emerge. It is this final assumption which seems likely to turn out to have been false.

I note that 'flexibility' and 'precariousness' are not the same thing, and neither of them is the same thing as the 'variety' which in an earlier section I discussed as a desideratum of human action (p. 106). To call what is actually 'precarisation' of employment 'flexibility of the labour market' is a classic instance of ideological obfuscation. That is, it uses a morally neutral or even mildly positive term, such as 'flexible', to cover over something which, if seen correctly, would not obviously recommend itself to us, namely a radical lack of job security. To say that I would like to be able to move freely between a number of activities is obviously not to say that I am happy to have no security in a job that I in some sense 'need'.

Outsourcing and Amazonisation

A further development in the world of work is the growth of outsourcing. In the first instance, outsourcing refers to changes in the structure of enterprises. They now no longer themselves do some of the things which they used to do, but rather have these hived off and done by separate, institutionally distinct, other firms. Thus, a publisher that used to employ a staff of its own – in-house – to evaluate manuscripts, copy-edit them, proof-read and index them, print them, and then distribute them to bookshops, now no longer employs copy-editors or printers of its own, but has its manuscripts looked after by a different company specialising in editorial services, and has them printed by independent printers. One certain effect of outsourcing will be an increase in informational and transaction costs. Now, for instance, at the very least formal contracts will have to be drawn up between press and printers, whereas before these could be dispensed with. More work, then, but for the lawyers. Experience also suggests that quality control also often suffers when too much of a firm's activity is outsourced.

From one point of view, outsourcing is just the latest instance of a tendency that is widespread in our economic system. One might even say that it is the central pillar of our form of free enterprise, the logic of which is to externalise the costs as much as possible, while appropriating any profits. Let the state build and maintain the road to the factory located on a river, and also let it clean up the pollution to the water supply that results, while the factory-owners appropriate whatever profit the factory turns.

The amazonisation of commerce takes this process one step further. This is a way of radically delocalising buying and selling. Businesses devoted to buying and selling at a distance take advantage of the possibilities for large-scale monopolisation offered by electronic media, primarily the internet, and by low transport costs. The electronic media depend completely on technologies that were developed over decades, mostly by governments at the tax-payer's expense (the British military during World War II, the US military during the Cold War, and the EU-funded research institute CERN); without massive financial support by governments over decades, such things as the internet would have been utterly impossible and would never have been developed. Commerce at a distance also requires transport costs to be kept low, and that is possible only because various states build and maintain such structures as the public roads, harbours, and airports, and also because they adopt political measures like the exemption of aviation fuel from taxation. This large-scale dependence on public monies is not usually something that these commercial enterprises are keen to emphasise. They prefer to pretend that they arise out of the inchoate fumblings of adolescents in a garage, who, relying on their own sheer genius alone, invent something out of nothing that changes the world. Low transport costs have a threefold advantage for these firms. First, they make it possible to ship to customers anywhere in the world, at very low cost to themselves; second, they allow a firm to locate its distribution centres in economically deprived areas where rents for premises and prevailing wages are low; and third, they keep the workforce (and the local government) docile, because the firm can very easily relocate if it is dissatisfied with the workers or the tax-regime. The enterprises themselves can quickly become so very large-scale, internally convoluted, and interlocked with other enterprises that they become unsurveyable and unpoliceable. They massively siphon off resources from communities and inflict permanent harm on local businesses, and once they have killed off local competition they may with some semblance of justification claim to have become effectively indispensable. Because they depend on low transport costs, which in turn depend on underpricing and low (or non-existent) rates of taxation on fossil fuels, businesses like Amazon are also ecologically destructive.

Ideology

Ideologically, it is striking that in many domains, categories derived from 'work' (or 'industry') are gradually being replaced by those derived from 'business'. That is, for a while work was the model of serious activity and was very positively valued, so some attempt was made to fit everything into the mould of (specifically industrial) labour. Thus, studying, teaching, and research was construed as 'academic work' (much to the hilarity, to be sure, of many of my co-workers in the steel mill: 'He calls "reading" "work"'), and there is a trace of this still operating in the attempt by people in theatre, film, and television, and to some extent writers, to construe themselves as working in the 'creative *industries*'. Nowadays, though, there is more likely to be an attempt to force those human activities that are particularly highly valued into the category of 'business'.

One should not attribute to this ideological difference more weight than it actually has. After all, even US Steel was always not just an industry but a business, and would always have freely admitted this, in fact gloried in it. Still, construing it as basically an industry means that there is at least lip-service paid to the priority of the quality of a product being produced. A businessman is unlikely to *say* explicitly 'and by the way what we deal in is crap', but the shift of focus is not insignificant. A colleague of mine who teaches in a well-known business school told me that when he asked, in the first class of the year, 'What is the point of the economy?,' he now invariably got the response 'To make money'. This, at least, is a different answer from the one

I would have got in Fairless Works, where the point of the factory was, at least ostensibly, 'To make steel'.

Part of our conception of waged labour is that people get a salary because they do something strenuous that is socially necessary, or at any rate useful. This conception is often moralised by filtering it through the language of 'merits' or 'deserts'. If a person does something strenuous that is socially necessary, she *deserves* her salary. Once the general idea of a close connection, especially a close normative connection, between a salary and strenuous, socially useful work gets established, it is possible for the tail to begin to wag the dog in either of two ways.

The first way for this to happen is for focus to fall on the moral or physical strenuousness of what some person has done,[11] as if that in itself gave a claim to deserve remuneration. Of course, numerous examples immediately spring to mind that suggest that this approach cannot be right. Some slave-catchers, interrogators, con-men, and hedge-fund managers work very hard, but does that imply that they deserve remuneration? If I am a pianist and cut off one finger before I begin to play the *Hammerklavier* sonata, do I increase my merit because I have made my task so much harder?

We might actually think that this whole project of studying the anthropology or the psychology of work – investigating whether people are really naturally lazy or whether they are active, or under what circumstances they feel themselves motivated to work hard and so forth – is itself, as a project, constantly in danger of falling into a trap, so that instead of being potentially a contribution to human enlightenment, it actually fosters an illusion that is central to capitalism's self-understanding. This is the illusion that riches are generally the result of hard work, and the strenuousness of the work in some sense gives a moral entitlement to the wealth. It is 'deserved'. The flip side of this is that those who are completely destitute, or even just poor, are generally in that state because they are lazy and undeserving.

If we had all lived for the past 2,000 or so years in Hesiod's world of more-or-less-equal small Mediterranean farmers, then perhaps *part* of the reason why farmer X, one season, prospered, whereas farmer Y did not, would be that X was stronger or more skilled than Y, or simply worked harder.[12] Another part of the story, of course, would be differences in the soil, in the weather, accidents of health during sowing and harvesting time, the number of children each could marshal to help with the work, which farm the pirates picked, almost at random, to raid when they landed, and so on. When Hesiod says that 'potter is angry with potter and builder with builder' he is also imagining a world of competition on terms of rough equality: one potter with a manually driven wheel and a bit of mud as against another with the same equipment, rather than Exekias the Potter against Royal Limoges or Porzellan-Manufaktur Meißen. Does a small computer company actually ever compete on terms of equality with Google?

It is overwhelmingly the case that how wealthy a person is today has nothing to do with his or her exertion or merit, but with history and luck. Maybe some ancestor worked hard and accumulated, but more characteristically fortunes arise from things like land-grabs (the enclosures of the late Middle Ages), the acquisition for a pittance of monastic property during the Reformation, slave-trading, the exploitation of historical accidents (oil discoveries), coercively enforced monopolies (on salt in India), or warfare (the Opium Wars fought to force China to sell us their tea for our [Indian] opium, not for silver). These were necessary to create a docile, needy, dependent work-force and to open markets for exploitation. If one is interested in normative assessment, none of these practices, which are at best highly dubious and at worst downright unsavoury, could be the foundation of any kind of plausible claim to merit or desert at all. If wealth usually resulted directly from hard work, then it might be important to know why some people were motivated to work hard, and others not, but if the relation of wealth and hard work is adventitious, why study motivation at all?

The second way in which the tail can come to wag the dog is to start not from the strenuousness of what a worker does, but from the salary itself. It might seem that anything for which one gets a salary is – in fact, must be – socially necessary or useful, or at any rate thought to be socially useful. After all, what could it possibly mean to say that some product or some service is socially useful other than that somebody wants the product or service, and what better sign can there be of that than that someone is willing to pay for it? So the fact that somebody is willing to pay a high salary to people doing a certain job shows that it makes a real, in fact a large, contribution to society.

This argument makes sense only if we systematically refuse to discriminate among different kinds of human wants, desires or preferences, and in particular makes no distinction between:

1. 'I want/desire X'
2. 'I will pay for X'
3. 'X is objectively (or, socially) necessary, useful, valuable.'

All three of these are basically to be treated as if they were the same thing. 'We *need* hospitals' really just means 'We want/wish/desire to have hospitals,' and that want or preference is on the same level as 'I like tea rather than coffee.' If nothing is allowed to be considered to be objectively needed (whether we know it or not) or objectively useful/good (whether we know it or not), then we must simply let all these wants and preferences fight it out, and God (in the form of the 'free market') will sort out which preferences are stronger and which, then, 'deserve' to prevail. This is known as 'rationality' or 'efficiency'.

Bullshit

In an important recent book, *Bullshit Jobs*,[13] to be sure, David Graeber analyses a phenomenon which throws a different light on the rationality of our economic system. This is the phenomenon of bullshitisation: the creation of more and more jobs that have no content and make no contribution to anything. Graeber's examples are the innumerable consultants, advisers, and managers of all kinds who have proliferated in every part of the economy, researchers in think-tanks, telemarketers, most people involved in finance, and most IT-providers (pp. 22–23). He formulates three criteria for calling something a 'bullshit job' (pp. 6–10):

(a) the job is pointless, unnecessary, or pernicious
(b) part of the job is to maintain the pretence that it is not pointless
(c) the people who perform it, themselves think it is useless.

It is hard to imagine anything more soul-destroying than the conjunction of uselessness and pretence. It should be a matter of amazement that many such jobs are, in fact, well paid and that their numbers seem to be inexorably increasing all the time. This trend – the constant and seemingly unstoppable creation of new useless jobs – runs directly counter to what is taking place in the sphere of employment as a whole, where the movement is in the direction of allowing automation (in its two forms, *vide supra*) to lead to the massive destruction of jobs.

The jobs that are now being abolished are such things as, for instance, those of supermarket cashiers who are being replaced by automated checkout systems, or those of the above-mentioned hotel chambermaids who are being made redundant by a new regime of intensification of work which allows fewer workers to do the same amount of work (or more). The lost jobs are said to be 'inefficient' (or at any rate they have now become less efficient than what supplants them), but no one could have claimed that they were not in some sense real jobs – human cashiers were not, the last time I looked, simply loafing their way through eight hours of work. Whatever else was true of them, they visibly contributed to the provision of a service. Furthermore, although it may well have been the case that before the introduction of new efficiency measures chambermaids were dissatisfied with various aspects of their work, they certainly didn't think it was pointless and useless – nor would the guests at the hotel have thought it was useless – and many of these workers wanted (all things considered) to keep their job.

If, however, it has proved to be relatively easy to abolish low-paid jobs which those who hold them really want to keep, and which visibly contribute to production, why should it be so hard to limit useless but well-paid bullshit jobs which those who occupy them hate? The observation that this is the case should in itself, as Graeber points out, put paid once and for all to the idea that there is some special, particularly fine-tuned efficiency associated with our economic system.

Graeber adopts a completely deadpan, non-judgemental attitude toward the jobs he discusses, making no assessment of his own about their value (see his condition (c) above). As he rightly remarks, if even the people who hold bullshit jobs and are well paid for performing them think they are pointless, then isn't that enough? Aren't they likely to know best?[14] That is all perfectly correct, but it shouldn't mean that in all contexts we are obliged to accept blindly the testimony of those who think that their job is wonderful, makes the wheels go around, and contributes greatly to human welfare. If there are that many people who know that their jobs are unnecessary or pernicious (and suffer from that), how many more will there be who are not fully aware of this, or simply do not care, or even take a perverse pleasure in their own uselessness? I would like to drop Graeber's condition (c) above, and use the term 'bullshit job' more widely than he does, so as to include even pointless, unnecessary, or pernicious jobs that people who perform them think are highly useful, which they might actually enjoy doing, and with which they might even strongly identify. That immediately raises the issue, which for Graeber doesn't arise at all: how I can justify claiming that something which some people enjoy doing – those who like their bullshit jobs – and other people are willing to pay to have done – the employers who create and fund the bullshit jobs – is actually or objectively pointless and useless?

This is a very good question which it is right to try to answer head on; it also, I think, raises an important point about the general relation between, to put it slightly pretentiously, the subjective and the objective in thinking about human society. No one is naive enough to take what people *say* as an infallible indication of what they think – sometimes they lie and sometimes they misspeak themselves. Even more importantly, sometimes they are simply mistaken. They say, for instance, with perfect sincerity that they want to do X, but their actions over a long period of time and in a wide variety of contexts show that they never show the slightest tendency to do X when they have ample opportunity. This is one of the reasons why any attempt to do social science exclusively on the basis of, say, questionnaires or interviews is never going to get one very far. This does not, of course, mean that one should simply ignore what people say about their beliefs and preferences, just that in some contexts, such as when we want certain kinds of understanding, we need to treat what they say as just one element – an important one, to be sure, but not the only one – that needs to be considered. People sometimes say, in interviews, surveys, or questionnaires, what they think they are supposed to say rather than what they really think. This is particularly true in the case of surveys about the workplace. Workers could well fear, rightly or wrongly, that they will be censured if they give the 'wrong' answer, and since many firms try desperately to maintain an upbeat image of themselves as providing a happy workplace full of contented employees, the outcomes of interviews or surveys can be biased. This, naturally, is only one of the many possible ways in which results from this kind of investigation can be seriously skewed. In addition, the job-holders' sincerely expressed views of the function and value of their work need not be the absolute and final word on the job's meaning, value, and general usefulness.

I know it is very unfashionable to claim that we must allow ourselves to make an independent assessment of the usefulness of jobs, just as we make an independent assessment of whether what one of our friends *says* he wants is something that he really wants. But if we aren't blind, we must allow ourselves in some contexts to say 'That job, as management consultant (or systems expert or whatever), is completely pointless, although the consultant (or expert or whatever), a pleasant enough young woman, is convinced she is doing something really useful,' just as we allow ourselves to say 'Jim keeps talking about how much he wants to learn Spanish, but here he is living in Mexico for the second year now with time on his hands and a housekeeper who speaks only a few words of English, and he makes no attempt to learn the language. Perhaps his desire isn't as strong as he thinks it is.' The reasons for saying what we say in either of these two cases will be highly contextual – they will refer to specific facts about the situation – but they need not be wilful or arbitrary. It is a *fact* that Jim has lived in Mexico, that he still does not speak Spanish, and so forth.

There are two, perhaps related, reasons to resist the idea that we could adopt an objective view about which jobs are useful and which not. The first is a kind of guilt by association. Ferenc Fehér and Agnes Heller described the Soviet-style regimes in Eastern Europe as 'dictatorships over needs'.[15] These were regimes in which the central government simply took it upon itself to decide what the population needed, which jobs were useful and which were not, and which consumer desires would be catered for and which would not. Of course, it was not the case that the governments in question took absolutely no account of what people said they wanted or needed, or which jobs they thought were useful and which were not. However, such opinions were subjected to a powerful process of filtration and transformation in which the political interests of the Party played a very important role, before they reached the central planners. I merely note that a rejection of Soviet-style political arrangements does not in itself in any way invalidate the general idea that there is some way of judging what people really want and what jobs are actually useful, independently of what those directly involved themselves say or think about the matter.

The second objection is more serious. When one says 'pointless and useless' this always means 'pointless and useless' *from someone's point of view*. If objective usefulness does not exist, and 'objectivity' itself is a construct, it is nonetheless also true that existing powerful agents will have a vested interest in, and often the power to enforce, their own monopolisation of this construct. This still does not mean that it is impossible to stand back from job-holders' own views about their job and assess its usefulness in a way that does not simply pander to the interests of the established political and economic agents. This is not an impossible, only a very difficult, and highly political, process.

Because this is all very abstract, let me give a couple of examples. Anyone who has worked in a large corporation during the past thirty years or so will be familiar with the 'training seminar'. These are usually given by highly paid independent consultants to people already at work in the corporation, and attendance at them is often mandatory for all members of staff. My own experience suggests that they are mostly a complete waste of time, and most of the people I know whose judgement I take seriously agree with this assessment. Now on what basis could I conceivably say that, if the person organising the seminar thinks he or she is doing something useful, and the people paying for it (usually the management of the corporation) think it is value for money? Well, perhaps I can't; that will depend on circumstances, and not absolutely *all* training sessions are a complete waste of time. Suppose, however, that regardless of the opinions of the seminar-leader or of management, all of the staff unanimously thinks the exercise was pointless, and can explain in great detail why they think that: the seminar-leader was unfamiliar with the realities of work of the kind this corporation does, the leader spouted trivialities which were well known to everyone in the room, the seminar was just part of a ploy on the part of the management to protect itself against possible lawsuits that actually resulted from its own ineptitude and not from anything the staff did, and so on. I as an independent observer can try to assess these claims, and I might find them to be the sorts of things that many people would find to be well-grounded. Similarly, I could independently investigate the staff itself and see whether it was composed of people who could explain their own jobs comprehensibly to me, had some results of their own work to point to, and were generally considered to be judicious, reliable, and effective at their job. None of this will result in a syllogistic proof that the seminar-leader is wrong to think the seminar had some value, because definitive proofs are in any case unavailable in this area, and so this is no objection. It is, of course, also the case that drawing the conclusion that we are in the presence of bullshit is a political act. It does not follow, however, that it is arbitrary, stipulative, merely subjective, or just my opinion. It can be supported by the various grounds I can cite for it, and which we can discuss, just as we can rationally discuss the merits of different forms of traffic regulation, taxation schemes, or reforms of the public school system.

Let me contrast this with another case. Any foreigner who has visited Japan will be struck by the wide variety of jobs which exist there but would certainly not exist in the West. I am thinking of the uniformed men with white gloves who stand at the top and bottom of the escalators in train stations to help people step on to and off the escalator, or the young women who greet customers when they enter large shops. There are also an amazing number of small 'granny' businesses (my term), even in urban centres. These are minuscule shops, found on every side street, in which an elderly man, or more frequently I think woman, offers a tiny selection of objects (soap, tobacco, tooth-brushes, sweets) for sale. What is even more surprising for a Westerner is that the people who have these jobs seem to take a great pride in what they are doing. They do not give the impression of being at all demoralised, and they seem to be treated with respect. They are at the other end of the spectrum from the standard urban taxi-driver whom one encounters in New York, Berlin, Paris, or London, and who characteristically seems to be a quivering mass of resent-ments only waiting to explode. As a foreigner one cannot easily judge whether the appearance of dignity and pride is real or merely superficial. On the other hand, what exactly would that distinction between appearance and reality mean in this case? If they comport themselves with dignity and are treated by others with dignity, isn't this sufficient? None of my Japanese friends ever suggests that any of these workers is eaten up by a secret sense of being declassé simply by virtue of working at this job. I have been told that the Japanese government made a decision after the war to give financial support (in the form of tax breaks) to these granny businesses because it was good for the neighbourhood to have a network of such deeply locally rooted shops, and it was good for members of the population, who were perhaps elderly or slightly infirm but not completely incapacitated, to have something to do. I would be disinclined to view any of these jobs as being pointless or mere bullshit. The escalator-men and the grannies in their shops are clearly providing a real service, not just doing something valueless or imaginary, and both they and virtually everyone else think that what they are doing is worthwhile. The same, in fact, is true about the greeters: why are they less useful than receptionists or doormen? What reason would one have to deviate from the social shared sense that these are proper jobs?

This still leaves an unresolved puzzle which is so extraordinary that it bears restating: large corporations seem to be destroying at great speed a huge number of real jobs – jobs that make some contribution to the business the corporation is purportedly engaged in – while at the same time creating many, often highly paid, bullshit jobs. If I understand Graeber correctly, he thinks that envy plays an important explanatory role here; at any rate many of his informants express this view to him. People actually very much want to do real, serious, productive work that allows them to deploy their skills to the full: they want to do good jobs as mechanics, engineers, builders, doctors, teachers, cooks – even, as I can attest from direct personal experience, as lowly cleaners. It follows that the people who have such jobs are the objects of great envy in a society which cannot provide everyone with a fulfilling job. What this means is that as organisations grow and are subject to the economic and, especially, financial imperatives that operate in our society, and as they tend to become more and more hierarchical, those directly in charge are forced to engage increasingly in activities that are divorced from any direct productive work. Depending on the particular conjunction of circumstances that holds, they will become merely ruthless extractors of profit, glad-handing smiley faces to charm potential investors or potential regulators, or the unavowed, subordinate henchmen of powerful economic agents which are in fact completely beyond their control. Under these circumstances, it would not be strange for many of them to feel resentment. Directing that against the economic system which constrains them in this way would for obvious reasons be a dangerous thing for them to do, so the hatred is directed against those who actually do something more than smile and enforce, namely against people who have real jobs in which they can deploy their skills to make something useful or provide a service that people really want and need. One can imagine a chairman of the board or chief executive officer (CEO) in a reflective moment, musing 'I have to sit around and deal with these finance people, these potential investors or these regulators all day long, and *you* actually get to *do stuff*. And you want to be *paid* for that, too? That's unfair. I'll at least make it my business to devalue what you are doing as much as possible, by seeing to it that your pay and your prestige are kept low, by reducing your numbers as much as I possibly can, by requiring ever more work from you under worse and worse working conditions, by inventing better paid (but useless) jobs placed in a hier- archy above you, and by burdening you, too, with as much bullshit as I can manage to throw at you.' By the creation of bullshit jobs, the CEO effectively devalues real work, thereby making himself feel better about his own uselessness. This account presupposes that the larger corporations in which the phenomenon of bullshitisation took root were actually generating sufficiently large profits to support the bullshit, and also that their organisational structure was sufficiently hierarchical that those at the top could actually make such a costly and far-reaching decision. Once, of course, the creation of bullshit jobs got established in a few high-visibility enterprises, the situation could change radically, because of the desire on the part of other corporations to imitate apparently highly successful firms. Having a mass of drones would be a status-symbol, a visible way of showing that one's own firm was solvent and up to date.

Politics

There are two wild cards in the situation I have described above, that is, two unknown factors that may well turn out to be crucial for what happens. First of all, I have assumed that advanced modern societies will continue to make some kind of at least minimal provision for the welfare of disabled, retired, or unemployed workers, and that we shall not revert to the brutal regimes that were in force before Bismarck's landmark introduction of social security in Germany beginning in 1883. Provision of welfare has been under sharp and constant attack, however, especially during the last forty years. One of the more seemingly plausible arguments has been that 'we can no longer afford to operate this kind of support for the economically inactive; it is just too expensive for us', but this strikes me as yet another political argument hiding behind a claim of 'economic necessity'. Since the 1980s many governments in Europe and North America have allowed a large part of their commerce to be monopolised by 'amazonised' structures which destroy local businesses and pay virtually no tax, and they have privatised public services according to the formula 'The private provider appropriates any profit, while the state covers infrastructure support, gives subsidies, and will provide a financial bail-out if things go wrong.' In addition, governments have refused to tax wealth or to impose a tax on financial transactions (Tobin tax), while maintaining taxes on income at historically low levels, and have made only token efforts to close down the large number of off-shore tax-havens where the wealthy can store their money with no questions asked. Under these circumstances, it is not surprising that the provision of welfare by the state has come under financial pressure. I merely point out that all of these were political decisions, and claims that they either boosted efficiency or were a response to an economic imperative are plausible only if one antecedently identifies 'efficiency' and 'economic imperative' precisely with the desire of private investors to have the highest possible short-term profits, whatever the consequences for the rest of society.

If, for whatever reason, workers' compensation, unemployment insurance, and related benefits are really all but abolished, this will be likely to reintroduce a virulence into the politics of work of a kind that has not been seen in the West for a long time.

Two Stories about the Future

The possible collapse of the welfare state was one wild card. The other is the possible collapse of our environment. To put it bluntly, for work to have a future, organised human society must have one, too, and at the moment that is not at all a foregone conclusion. It seems clear that the world cannot continue to sustain the current human population at anything like its present level of resource use. Furthermore, even to speak of the 'present level of resource use' is misleading because it leaves out what is one of the most salient aspects of the way resources are used around the world, namely that it is characterised by gross inequalities. These inequalities are partly geographic and partly class-related. The average citizen in North America or in Europe uses many times as much energy as the average person in a poorer region, and in every region the rich use more than the poor; that is what it is to be 'rich'. I assume that at least at a very superficial level it will be generally accepted that we are gradually using up essential, unrenewable resources in an unsustainable way, destroying the environment, and poisoning ourselves. Starting from this observation, there are basically two kinds of possible stories one can tell about what it is reasonable to expect from the future, each based on a slightly different set of hypotheses. The first is a deeply pessimistic story: there was nothing inherently doomed about our industrial society. If in the 1960s and early 1970s when we became globally aware of the problems, we had devoted all of our technical and scientific expertise to changing our modes of production, and all of our social and political skills to changing our mode of living, it might very well have been possible to avoid ever finding ourselves in the situation we are now in. We would perhaps have needed to adopt universal vegetarianism, completely banned private cars, reduced air traffic to some small fraction of what it is now, practised draconian population limitation, and implemented half a dozen other significant changes in the way we live, combining these with massive programmes of cleaning up the oceans, reforestation, and decarbonisation through the development of solar and wind energy (and so forth). There was nothing inherently impossible about that; it would just have been inconvenient and would have required a political consensus that did not exist. For whatever reason, we didn't do any of these things and so we missed that crucial moment, and now it is fifty years too late. The world's population has more than trebled and global warming, climate change, desertification, and pollution have now reached levels which we could not deal with even if we wanted to look at them realistically and try. If the situation really is beyond our control, there is no point in adding to that a sense of panic. We can, if we wish, do various things to make ourselves feel better and calmer as our circumstances get progressively worse, and perhaps working is as good a way as any, but that does not mean that even assiduous work will have any final effect on either our individual or our collective chances of survival, which are minimal or non-existent.

That is the first kind of story one can tell about our probable future. The second, in contrast, is much more upbeat, emphasising the prospects for continued technological advance which will eventually allow us to cope with our deteriorated ecological situation. We can expect, this story would run, there to be a series of three or four technological 'miracle' discoveries which will allow us, at any rate those of us in the industrialised West, to continue with only a minor reduction in our population and our levels of consumption. The reason why we should be confident is that we have always in the past found a technological trick to avoid predicted catastrophe. The often-predicted shortage of oil has not materialised; vaccines have eventually been discovered for most major epidemic illnesses; Malthus – whose analysis seemed to imply a future of increasing mass starvation as population outstripped agricultural output – turned out not to be a very good guide to what would happen in Europe in the nineteenth and twentieth centuries. Something, some technological fix, always turns up. Is this simple induction or advanced Micawberism?

In our own particular situation time is of the essence. For the optimistic scenario to be plausible, not only must it be the case that some miracle solution to our environmental problems turns up, but it must turn up in time because the clock is ticking. One way to see the future, then, is as a race between the search for a big technological fix and the progressive process of ecological degradation. Will the fix (if it exists) be found before the air, water, and soil of the planet become irrevocably toxic? In fact, of course, if catastrophe strikes, it will not necessarily be in the form of asphyxiation from the exhaust fumes of our own vehicles – it is more likely to be the result of political attempts to deal with shortages. The foresight which humans have is limited, uncertain, and motivationally weak, and we are as a species disorganised, but the predictive powers of individual countries are sufficiently operational to make it likely that they will become very aggressive as resources run out. It is little consolation that wars and massacres are likely to kill more people than exhaust fumes, heat-stroke, or starvation.

Conclusion

A specific configuration of ideas has dominated our thinking about our social and individual life for a very long time. One central component of that configuration is the assumption that most of the population must engage in a form of work which is modelled on what peasant agriculturalists did for millenia or industrial labourers did for centuries. It seems unlikely that this collection of beliefs and associated attitudes can continue to have the same relevance as it once had. Food production and some industrial (or at any rate craft) activity will need to continue for as long as humans survive, and we don't know how they will be organised, but barring a form of catastrophe which leaves many of us alive but our society completely demechanised, human participation in these activities will be much reduced, if not absolutely minimal. Perhaps there will be some services that need to be performed by human beings rather than robots, but the bulk of the population will be detached from this. (And I also note that it was precisely those jobs which were considered safe from mechanisation, jobs which most people prefer to have done by other people, such as hairdressing, that were most affected by the pandemic in 2020.) How individuals acquire the means for living will be highly varied, fragmented, and adventitious. Maybe most of us will go back to something like the post-industrial equivalent of hunting and gathering, pursuing opportunistically whatever odd jobs, forms of mutual aid, charity, or kinds of partial governmental support happen to be available in a given place at a given time, just as the members of a band might have survived by gathering what berries were in season, pursuing whatever game happened to be around, and exchanging goods with the occasional member of another band whom they might happen to meet. Or will we have a form of war communism?[16]

We don't know how society will deal with the fact that – suddenly or gradually – what we would now call 'unemployment' will not be in some sense an aberration, or misfortune, affecting different individual sectors of the population at different times and with different intensity, but rather will be the permanent state of most people. No one has any experience of organising a society like that: how will food be distributed? How will people be chosen to be doctors and technicians? How will they be trained?

One thing we have to learn is how to be meaningfully active while producing and consuming less, and while freeing ourselves completely from the pathologies of infinite growth and of the ever-increasing development of human productive powers. The elements that came together to make up the traditional conception of work – the idea that most of the population will be engaged in the strenuous production of necessities organised into a series of jobs – have now separated, dissociated themselves from each other, and dispersed, and many of them have changed so much that they are scarcely recognisable at all. Where we go now, if we survive long enough to be said to 'go' anywhere, is anybody's guess.

SUGGESTED FURTHER READING

What follows is a list of works which bear on the topic of work. I have given priority to work available in English.

Indispensable Classics

Émile Durkheim, *The Division of Labour in Society* (Free Press, 1997)

G. W. F. Hegel, *Hegel's Phenomenology of Spirit* (Oxford University Press, 1970)

Karl Marx, *Capital: A Critique of Political Economy*, Vol. I (Penguin, 1990)

Karl Marx and Friedrich Engels, *Economic and Philosophical Manuscripts of 1844* (Progress Publishers, 1959)

Karl Marx and Friedrich Engels, *The German Ideology* (Progress Publishers, 1964)

Adam Smith, *An Inquiry into the Nature and Cause of the Wealth of Nations*, ed. R. H. Campbell and A. S. Skinner (Liberty Fund, 1982)

Max Weber, *The Protestant Ethic and the Spirit of Capitalism* (Oxford University Press, 2010)

Interesting More Recent Works

Luc Boltanski and Ève Chiapello, *The New Spirit of Capitalism*, translated by G. Elliott (Verso, 2006)

Le comité invisible, *The Coming Insurrection* (MIT Press, 2009)

André Gorz, *Critique of Economic Reason* (Verso, 1989)
David Graeber, *Bullshit Jobs* (Simon & Schuster, 2018)
Ivan Illich, *Shadow-Work* (Marion Boyars, 1981)
Peter Kropotkin, *Mutual Aid: A Factor of Evolution* (Freedom Press, 2009)
Adolf Loos, *Ornament and Crime* (Penguin, 2019)
Brian O'Connor, *Idleness* (Princeton University Press, 2018)

Literature

Hesiod, *Works and Days*, translated by M. L. West (Oxford University Press, 2008)
Vergil, *Georgica*, translated by C. D. Lewis (Oxford University Press, 1999)
Émile Zola, *Germinal* (Penguin, 2004)
Anton Platonov, *Foundation-Pit* (New York Review of Books, 2009)
Michel Houellebecq, *The Map and the Territory* (Knopf, 2010)

Further Philosophical Reflections

Simone de Beauvoir, 'Pyrrhus and Cineas', in *Philosophical Writings* (University of Illinois Press, 2014)
John Dewey, *Art as Experience* (Perigee, 1934)
Johann Fichte, *The Closed Commercial State* (State University of New York Press, 2013)
Martin Heidegger, 'A Letter on Humanism', in *Basic Writings*, ed. D. Farrell Krell (Harper Collins, 1977)
Paul Lafargue, *The Right to Be Lazy* (Andesite Press, 2015)

History and Anthropology

Henry Mayhew, *London Labour and the London Poor*, abridged edition (Oxford University Press, 2012)

George Orwell, *Down and Out in Paris and London* (Penguin, 2001)

George Orwell, *The Road to Wigan Pier* (Penguin, 2001)

Marshall Sahlins, *Stone-Age Economics* (Aldine, 1972)

James Scott, *Against the Grain* (Yale University Press, 2018)

Studs Terkel, *Working* (Pantheon, 1974)

Chapter 1

1 See David Graeber, *Debt: The First 5000 Years* (Melville House, 2011).
2 *Marx-Engels-Werke* (Dietz, 1960), Ergänzungsband 1, pp. 510–522.
3 Heinrich Heine, *Reisebilder. Späte Lyrik* (Goldmann, 1957), p. 201.
4 Plato, *The Apology of Socrates*.

Chapter 2

1 Max Weber, *Wirtschaft und Gesellschaft* (Mohr, 1972), pp. 126–130.
2 One might suspect that the theological or ontological assumption has been replaced by one which makes the economic system the vengeful deity. If the society is ruthless and survival difficult, it might be highly unwise not to cultivate those abilities one has which are economically rewarded.
3 Friedrich Nietzsche, *Werke: Kritische Studienausgabe*, ed. G. Colli and M. Montinari (de Gruyter, 1980), Vol. 5, pp. 291–337.
4 This is true only for relatively small debts. As has often been pointed out, for huge debts, the relation may be reversed. If I owe you €1,000, this gives you leverage over me; if I owe a bank €1 billion, I may have leverage over them, because if I don't repay them, they go bankrupt.

5 David Graeber, *Debt: The First 5000 Years* (Melville House, 2011).

6 James Scott, *Against the Grain* (Yale University Press, 2017), p. 71.

7 James Scott, *Against the Grain* (Yale University Press, 2017), p. 43–55.

8 Thomas Hobbes, *Leviathan* (Cambridge University Press, 1996), I.13.

9 Marshall Sahlins, *Stone-Age Economics* (Taylor & Francis, 1972).

10 Plato, *The Republic*, 343ff.

11 Montaigne, *Essais*, II.12.

Chapter 3

1 Michel Foucault, *Surveiller et punir* (Gallimard, 1975).

2 G. W. F. Hegel, *Werke*, ed. E. Muldenhauer and K. M. Michel (Suhrkamp, 1970), Vol. 7, pp. 442f., 467; Vol. 10, pp. 340–345; Vol. 12, pp. 444–446, 478; Vol. 19, pp. 542ff.; Vol. 12, pp. 527–531.

3 See Denys Page, *Sappho and Alcaeus* (Oxford University Press, 1955), p. 315.

4 Émile Durkheim, *De la division du travail* (Presses Universitaires de France, 1893).

5 See Bernard Williams, *Shame and Necessity* (University of California Press, 1993).

6 Hesiod, *Works and Days*, translated by M. L. West (Oxford University Press, 2008), lines 20–26.

7 Some try to discredit any call for egalitarianism as an expression of envy of those who are better off. The young Marx castigated the demand for equality arising from envy as a form of 'crude communism'. Managers, however, have no

qualms about trying to generate envy in their workforce by playing off one group against another. There can be good grounds to oppose extreme inequality of wealth in societies which permit that inequality to be translated into political power; these grounds may have nothing at all to do with envy. I may not envy Mr X if he has a house ten times bigger than mine. Yet if Mr X can buy a chain of newspapers and television stations, found think-tanks to propagate views he finds congenial, or attract all the best doctors to his private health scheme, these are material social evils that must be combatted by making certain forms of inequality impossible. This has nothing to do with envy. See also my 'Envy and the Politics of Identification', in Raymond Geuss, *Reality and Its Dreams* (Harvard University Press, 2016).

8 Mancur Olson, *The Logic of Collective Action* (Harvard University Press, 1965).

9 Friedrich Nietzsche, *Werke: Kritische Studienausgabe*, ed. G. Colli and M. Montinari (de Gruyter, 1980), Vol. 5, pp. 339–412.

10 Max Weber, *Gesammelte Aufsätze zur Religionssoziologie* (Mohr, 1920), Vol. I, p. 203.

11 Luc Boltanski and Ève Chiapello, *Le nouvel esprit du capitalisme* (Gallimard, 1999).

12 G. W. F. Hegel, *Werke*, ed. E. Muldenhauer and K. M. Michel (Suhrkamp, 1970), Vol. 13, p. 51. The motif recurs in Musset's *Lorenzaccio*, Act II, scene 6, where Lorenzaccio, who is observed while throwing the chain-mail of Duke Alexander into a well (in order to make him easier to assassinate), claims he was just spitting into the well to watch the circles that he could produce, this being his greatest pleasure. The point, presumably, is to make him seem childlike and inoffensive.

13 The eponymous protagonist of Ivan Goncharov's novel *Oblomov* (1859) was a pathologically indolent landowner.

14 John Locke, *Two Treatises of Government* (Cambridge University Press, 1988), Second Treatise, 2.28.

15 Bertolt Brecht, 'Fragen eines lesenden Arbeiters', in *Die Gedichte* (Suhrkamp, 1981), p. 656.

16 Arthur Rimbaud, *Œuvres complètes* (Gallimard, 1972), pp. 248–249; Friedrich Nietzsche, *Werke: Kritische Studienausgabe*, ed. G. Colli and M. Montinari (de Gruyter, 1980), Vol. 5, pp. 278–281.

Chapter 4

1 *Marx-Engels-Werke* (Dietz 1960), Ergänzungsband 1, pp. 518–519, 540–542.

2 G. W. F. Hegel, *Die Phänomenologie des Geistes*, ed. H.-F. Wessels and H. Clairmont (Meiner, 2006), p. 390.

3 *Marx-Engels-Werke* (Dietz 1960), Ergänzungsband 1, pp. 510–522.

4 Karl Marx, *Grundrisse der Kritik der politischen Ökonomie* (Dietz, 1974), p. 378.

5 Martin Heidegger, *Platons Lehre von der Wahrheit mit einem Brief über den Humanismus* (Franke, 1947), pp. 53–119.

6 Martin Heidegger, *Einführung in die Metaphysik* (Niemeyer, 1957), pp. 112–126.

7 Martin Heidegger, *Gelassenheit* (Klett-Cotta, 1959).

8 Voltaire, *Romans et Contes* (Gallimard, 1960), p. 221.

9 Humans do have a tendency to treat some things which we know to be inanimate objects as if they had interests of their own. Anthropologists used to speak about 'animistic' beliefs when they found members of pre-industrial societies attributing 'souls' to particularly numinous places, rock formations, rivers, winds or fetishes (like bundles of wood and feathers). People in our society who work for a long time in a

close relation of dependence on a machine that lends itself to personification, particularly a large machine that appears to move freely like an animal – a locomotive, lorry, or airplane – often speak of the machine as if it had a soul and interests of its own, for instance the locomotive driver who says of his engine 'Don't push her; she wants to stop now' or the secretary I knew who used to say about her electric typewriter 'She is always exhausted on Monday morning after a long weekend.' The conditions under which we project our own psychic states onto objects deserve a fuller treatment (including a treatment of their political dimension) than this book can offer.

10 See Ceylan Yeginsu, 'If Workers Slack Off, the Wristband Will Know It. (And Amazon Has a Patent for It.)', in *The New York Times*, 1 February 2018.

11 See the section on Physical and Moral Exertion in Chapter 1 (p. 9).

12 I note that the word used for Y in Hesiod is *apalamon*, which seems to be ambiguous as between 'unskilled' and 'unmotivated'. See Denys Page, *Sappho and Alcaeus* (Oxford, 1955), p. 315.

13 David Graeber, *Bullshit Jobs* (Allen Lane, 2018).

14 David Graeber, *Bullshit Jobs* (Allen Lane, 2018), pp. 10–16.

15 Ferenc Fehér and Agnes Heller, *Diktatur über die Bedürfnisse: Sozialistische Kritik osteuropäischer Gesellschaftformationen* (VSA Verlag, 1979).

16 Andreas Malm, *Corona, Climate, Chronic Emergency: War Communism in the Twenty-First Century* (Verso, 2020).

INDEX